Américo Paredes

In His Own Words, an Authorized Biography

Manuel F. Medrano

Number 5 in the
Al Filo: Mexican American Studies Series

University of North Texas Press
Denton, Texas

10 9 8 7 6 5 4 3 2

Permissions:
University of North Texas Press
1155 Union Circle #311336
Denton, TX 76203-5017

The paper used in this book meets the minimum requirements of the
American National Standard for Permanence of Paper for Printed Library
Materials, z39.48.1984. Binding materials have been chosen for durability.

Library of Congress Cataloging-in-Publication Data

Medrano, Manuel, 1949-
Américo Paredes : in his own words, an authorized biography / Manuel
F. Medrano, Jr. – 1st ed.
p. cm. – (Number 5 in the Al filo: Mexican American studies series)
Includes bibliographical references and index.
ISBN 978-1-57441-287-1 (cloth : alk. paper)
ISBN 978-1-57441-847-7 (paperback)
1. Paredes, Américo. 2. Mexican American authors–Texas–Biography. 3.
Authors, American–20th century–Biography. 4. Folklorists–Texas–
Biography. 5. Mexican Americans–Texas–Biography. I. Paredes, Américo.
II. Title. III. Series: Al filo ; no. 5.
PS3531.A525M43 2010
813'.54–dc22
[B]   2009050515

Design by Angela Schmitt

Américo Paredes: In His Own Words, an Authorized Biography is Number 5 in
the Al Filo: Mexican American Studies Series

CONTENTS

Illustrations after Page 74

PREFACE

The idea for this project was born in November 1998, after Américo Paredes had been honored with a tribute at the University of Texas at Brownsville. I had known of him since my high school days but I had not known him until I first interviewed him in September 1994. After the aforementioned tribute, I asked him if anyone was doing a book about his life. He replied that someone was writing about his works, but not about his life. Américo agreed to let me write his life story, but then died in May 1999, and I renegotiated with his sons Alan and Vince to continue the biography. Since then I have visited with them numerous times and they have generously agreed to be videotaped. The book is not an analysis of Paredes' works nor is it an examination of his academic or political philosophy, although they are mentioned. It is about him—a young man with an energy and a burning ambition to write and to succeed, a mature scholar with a determination to change the status quo, and a professor emeritus relentless in his research and respected by those he had taught, those he had trained, and those he had touched.

ACKNOWLEDGMENTS

Much of this book is a compilation of oral history interviews from Américo Paredes himself, from his family including his sons Alan and Vince, his brother, Lorenzo, his nieces Lydia and Blanca, and his nephews Manfred and Joe del Castillo. It is also a product of interviews with his colleagues and students including José Limón, Richard Flores, Jordanna Barton, Emilio Zamora, Francis Terry, José Angel Gutiérrez, Rolando Hinojosa, Antonio Zavaleta, the late federal Judge Reynaldo Garza and late historian Bruce Aiken. Finally it is a product of my recollections of Don Américo and my respect to the legacy he left. A significant amount of resource material was provided by the Américo Paredes Papers at the Nettie Lee Benson Library at the University of Texas at Austin. The librarians, especially Ms. Margot Gutiérrez and Mr. Michael Hironymous, were most helpful and patient.

At the University of Texas at Brownsville/Texas Southmost College my gratitude extends to President Juliet V. García; former Provost for Academic Affairs José Martin; English professor Farhat Iftekharuddin; Vice-President for Academic Affairs, Charles Dameron; and Associate Vice President Ethel Cantu; History Department Chairperson, Dr. Helmut Langerbein; friends and colleagues, Dr. Anthony Knopp and Dr. Denise Joseph and the rest of my History Department colleagues who constantly encouraged me. Gratitude extends also to my friends at the UTB/TSC Media Services, Mr. Ricardo Camargo, Mr. Juan Miguel Gonzalez, Mr. Gilbert Garza, Mr. Johnny Aguilar for their expertise, and to Mr. Norberto Martínez and Ms. Letty Fernandez from the Office of Public Information for their assistance. My gratitude also extends to Dr. Rolando Hinojosa, Dr. Teresa Cadena, Dr. José Garza, and Ms. Isabel de la Torre for taking the time to comment on the manuscript. Special thanks go to

Ms. Ana Liy Villalpando and especially to Ms. Monica Lerma and Ms. Martha Arias, who diligently assisted me with word processing and transcription. Additionally, my appreciation extends to Roberto R. Calderón, Ronald Chrisman, and Karen DeVinney for their editorial comments.

Finally, my highest regards go to my family—my wife, Chavela, my sons, Noe, Estevan and Daniel, my mother Antonia, my father Manuel and my brothers and sisters who through past and present have supported what I do.

INTRODUCTION

His first name was Américo, like the explorer for which America was named. His last name was Paredes, which comes from the Latin word *parietis* meaning walls. His life spanned eight decades that included events that changed the world forever. Américo Paredes was born September 3, 1915, during the devastation of World War I and the chaos of the Mexican Revolution, and died on Cinco de Mayo, 1999, on a day celebrating the battle of Puebla in Mexican history. He lived during some of most dramatic events in U.S. history: World War I, the Great Depression, World War II, and the Cold War.

Although he often wrote about life between two worlds, he lived in three: his world during the early years on the border; his world during and after World War II in the Far East; and his world of academia at The University of Texas at Austin. Throughout his life, he broke new ground in the face of resistant tradition. At a Brownsville tribute to him in 1998, his niece, Margot Torres, referred to him as "Don" Américo and explained why he deserved that distinction:

> In our culture, the word "Don" denotes greatness, and it is used as a title of a man who has reached the pinnacle of his career or life. When we use the word "Don," we had better be certain that the person truly deserves the title or the word becomes meaningless. Therefore, it is with great pride that I say tío, Don Américo Paredes, I will always hold you in very high

regard. You exemplify everything which I hold very
dear in life.[1]

Américo Paredes grew up between two worlds along the U.S./Mexico border: one written about in books and the other sung about in ballads and told in folktales.

He attended a school system that emphasized conformity and Anglo values in a town whose population was 70 percent Mexican in origin. By seventeen years of age, he was translating and writing poetry in newspapers and writing his first novel, *George Washington Gómez*. Soon after, he was a young journalist writing for newspapers such as *La Prensa*.

During World War II, he worked for the International American Red Cross and wrote for the *Stars and Stripes* army newspaper in the Far East. He returned to Texas with a new bride and a passion for continuing his formal education and his writing. Paredes did both at The University of Texas at Austin, completing his Ph.D. in 1956 and publishing his dissertation, under the title of *With His Pistol in His Hand* in 1958. Some criticized him for demanding too much of his students and too much of his family. Some disliked him simply because he was an agent of change.

For the next forty years, he was a brilliant teacher and prolific writer who championed the preservation of border culture and history. During his life, he learned five languages: Spanish, English, French, German, and Portuguese, expanding his ability to understand the complexity of various cultures including the culture of the border. Although typically quiet, he became temperamental about issues such as discrimination. He was a fearless professor who challenged the traditional accounts about the Texas Rangers and South Texas folklore.

By the end of his life, he was beloved by thousands whom he had taught and known as a respected scholar on two continents. For those who knew him, the passing of Américo Paredes was the end of a significant era in Mexican American history and a deep, personal loss. As a folklorist and maestro or teacher of the Texas Mexican corrido or folk ballad, he had few rivals. As a scholar who inspired with his knowledge and entertained with his humor, he had few equals. As a friend, he was unforgettable.

CHAPTER ONE
THE FORMATIVE YEARS

Historically, the South Texas frontera has been inhabited by Coahuiltecanos, Spaniards, Mexicanos, Tejanos and Anglo Americans and many others. A century before the founding of Paredes' hometown, haciendas, villas, and ranchos dotted the landscape on both sides of the Río Grande. Then, the llano and river united, rather than divided, a people.

In 1836 it belonged to the Republic of Texas, and nine years later, it became part of the state of Texas. Within a year, the U.S.-Mexican War began on this same soil claimed by both countries at the Battle of Palo Alto. By mid-August 1847 military hostilities ended in Mexico City and in early February 1848, the Treaty of Guadalupe Hidalgo was ratified. As a result, Mexico ceded nearly one-half of its territory and over eighty thousand Mexicanos living on it. Mexico emerged from this conflict debt-ridden and seeking new political leadership, while the United States faced further division over the slavery issue. Former Mexican territory was viewed by many as conquered land and the new Americans, formerly Mexicanos, as conquered people. As a result, cohabitation and economic and political maintenance of the area were, at times, marked by distrust and conflict.

Soon afterward Anglos established an interim government in the territories of the Mexican Cession and in Texas laid the foundation for future control. Arnoldo de Leon, Tejano scholar and author of *Mexican Americans in Texas,* asserts that this was generally achieved through mechanisms that maintained Anglo sovereignty. The first was the threat of or use of violence by both Anglos and Tejanos. A prime example was the Cart War of 1857 involving Tejano arrieros and Anglo freighters competing for control of the transportation of goods between San Antonio and the Gulf of Mexico. Two years later, the Cortina War erupted in Brownsville, led by the hero/bandit Juan N. Cortina. This conflict was preceded by a struggle for political and economic dominance. In 1877 the Salt War near El Paso produced an ethnic conflict over control of salt lodes, which were communally owned by Tejanos.

A second mechanism of control was interethnic accommodation that included tactical marriages between elite Tejanos and newly arrived Anglos. Although partially beneficial to landholding Tejano families, these marriages gave Anglos increased social and familial acceptance among Tejanos as well as ranch lands. Sovereignty was also achieved through political bossism and controlled franchise, usually preceded by "pachangas," pre-election political fiestas. Finally, Anglo control was maintained by the accumulation of large quantities of land, usually bought inexpensively at sheriffs' auctions. The owners were forced to sell their property either for back taxes, after being intimidated, or because of losses as a result of decreasing beef prices.[2]

Ethnic friction impacted by these mechanisms continued into the early twentieth century. The infamous Brownsville Raid of 1906, which resulted in the dishonorable discharge of African American soldiers stationed at Fort Brown with little firm evidence, attested to the federal government's racial attitudes and the racial and ethnic tension. A few years later, the demise of the Díaz government in Mexico and the ensuing Mexican Revolution only increased the discord. In short, the birthplace of Américo Paredes had a documentable history of ethnic conflict and violence.

His life began on the U.S./Mexico border, where cultures, customs, and languages merged and clashed. This was the place where he would learn the folklore and history that shaped his life. Paredes said, "I was born in Brownsville. I'm a Brownsville boy born

September 3, 1915, during the height of the border troubles when there was an ethnic cleansing, to use the current term, along the border when Texas Rangers and others murdered a number of Mexicans and forced many others to leave the country." [3]

It is only fitting that Américo Paredes' life began during a time of collective protest: a time of the Norias raid, of el Plan de San Diego and a time of *los sediciosos* (those who attempted a revolt to separate South Texas from the United States and to establish a separate republic). According to historian David Montejano, "the armed insurrection of Texas Mexicans and its brutal suppression by Texas Rangers... turned the Valley into a virtual war zone."[4] Throughout much of his life, Paredes himself protested the mistreatment of Mexicanos and Tejanos by the Rangers and others through his writings.

Paredes was born into a ranching family with a long history in northern Mexico. In June 1749 Don José Escandon commissioned Captain Don Pedro González de Paredes to lead fifty families to colonize a settlement called Villa de Bedoya on the Nueces River. Regrettably, Captain Paredes died on the banks of the Río Grande when his expedition was en route to el Río Nueces. As a result, the expedition was ordered to return to Soto la Marina.

Over a century and a half before, in 1580, José de Carvajal y de la Cueva brought a colony of Sephardic Jews to present-day Nuevo León; they had left Spain to escape religious persecution. Among them were more of the New World Paredes. Américo's family tree can be traced to the marriage of Don José María Paredes to Doña Gertrudis Ibarra in 1585. Originally from Abasolo, Don José moved his family to El Rosario Ranch and later, north of San Antonio River in the northern region of Nuevo Santander.

Don Américo's father, Justo Paredes Cisneros, was born in Matamoros, Tamaulipas, in November 1868. He was the oldest son of seven children. Paredes remembered this about his father: "My father was always a rebel. He joined Catarino Garza's revolt [an attempted northern uprising led by a journalist in 1891] against Díaz. He was wounded. Of course, his father [Américo's grandfather] had fought against the French. He was a supporter of Díaz so he arranged things to be settled.[5]

Justo later built a home across from his father's house and married. His first children were born on a rancho near Matamoros. In 1904, the family moved to Brownsville where Justo became the political boss. Paredes' mother, Cleotilde Manzano Paredes, was born in Bagdad, Tamaulipas, in June 1883. Bagdad, a small town near the mouth of the Río Grande, had been a boom town for trade during the Civil War.[6] Her father was born in the province of Asturias, Spain.

Américo's family history was like that of many whose ancestors came from Spain and settled in Nuevo Santander, the colony between the Nueces and Pánuco rivers. Eventually, some were victimized by the political, socioeconomic, and historical changes that erased some borders and created new ones. As a result, the lands that many owned changed hands. Alan Paredes, one of Américo's sons, later commented about the violence during that era:

> [I]t affected our family personally; he [Américo] had an uncle and I think it was an uncle that was riding on his ranch with his son, and this, you know, a posse of Texas Rangers came and started shooting at him, killed his uncle. And, of course, when we were kids we would watch the Texas Rangers on TV and it would infuriate him because they were all good guys in pressed shirts and nice shiny boots, and do-gooders. And my dad said that that might be true, but if you were a Mexican American back then you know then you got winged or shot a lot because of the color of your skin, because of who you were....[7]

Unlike many others who had their land stolen, Paredes' father Justo willingly transferred the title to the family land to a younger brother and moved his family to Brownsville. Américo Paredes was one of nine children. Four were born in Matamoros and five, including Américo, were born in Brownsville. His eldest brother, Eliseo, was born in 1899. His eldest sister, Isaura, was born in 1902, Lorenzo in 1904, Cleotilde in 1906, and Blanca in 1909. Justo was born in 1912, Américo in 1915 and the twins, Amador and Eleazar, in 1920.

Américo had some interesting recollections about his schooling and his childhood in Brownsville. In the early 1920s, there was only one grammar school in the city, later named Annie S. Putegnat Elementary, after a local long-time educator. Paredes remembered, "In the lower grades, 90 percent were Mexicans. So really the Anglos were a minority. Sometimes if they didn't watch out, they might be beaten up. Everyone spoke Spanish. They were not supposed to. I'm sure that began around World War I and was aimed at the Germans, not at the Mexicans."[8] His first-grade teacher was Ms. Josephine Castañeda, who was the sister of Carlos Castañeda, The University of Texas historian, who was born in Camargo, Tamaulipas, but who grew up in Brownsville. Castañeda attended St. Joseph's Academy, a Catholic school, with Américo's older brother, Lorenzo.

Américo Paredes recalled that although he and other Tejano students did not encounter too many problems at school, the new immigrant children whose families had been displaced by the Mexican Revolution were picked on. They either did not know the English language or spoke it with an accent.

It was during these early years that Américo first heard the word *mojado*. Paredes remembered, "It does not mean wetback, for god's sake. I remember them chasing one little boy yelling "mojado, mojado" [illegal, illegal] and knocked him down. They felt behind his ears. That is where they were supposed to be mojados."[9] Paredes continued by saying that the word became popular during the Prohibition Era. Since the pro-alcohol proponents were already called "wets," it was only logical to call undocumented Mexicans crossing the Río Grande by the Spanish translation of "wets": "mojados."

During Américo's high school years, J. Frank Dobie, a prominent Texas folklorist, became nationally known. With a facetious smirk on his face Paredes said, "He knew Mexicans better than they knew themselves."[10] Among the racist stories that Dobie told that Américo heard was one about mojados. Dobie said that Mexicans jumped into the river fully clothed because they were too dumb to undress. They swam across the river to the opposite side for a siesta. They would lie on their backs, and when they awakened, their clothes had dried except for their backs. That's why Mexicans were called wetbacks. "It stuck in my mind because it shows the prejudice and stereotype," said Paredes.[11] He later satirized Dobie as the historian and folklorist K. Hank Harvey in his novel *George Washington Gómez*. He met Dobie in 1950 when Paredes returned from the Far East. Years later, Paredes recalled that Dobie "wasn't such a bad guy. Sometimes, we feuded as far as Mexicans were concerned, but not in an offensive way."[12]

Paredes had an interesting comment about his middle school years at Central Junior High School. The 90 percent majority of Mexicans who had attended grammar school with him dropped out in large numbers. He recalled that in an ancient history class there were only four students, three Anglos and himself. The effects of the Depression and the challenges that kept most Mexicans from continuing their education beyond grade school were taking their toll. He remembered,

> As a young man, I had, of course, a lot of barrio friends, but most of them moved away and I moved away from them, too. I mean they dropped out of school. One of them herded goats instead because his father had a dairy. He was born in the house next to us on the same date when I was born… and, yet some times when I was grown, he would look me up and say, '¿Américo, cuántos años tenemos?' [Américo, how old are we?] He didn't even know how old he was—So my friends came from a considerable distance.[13]

Paredes remembered that during those years "Brownsville was like a little Mexican town"[14] with a population of less than 25,000. Families would walk on both sides of Elizabeth, the main street, and visit and shop on Saturday evenings. As the parents were talking, the young men and the young women would walk in groups emulating the *paseo* tradition of earlier times in Mexico. After this initial contact, the courtship would continue, sometimes including serenades and gifts until they married. This tradition continued throughout the 1920s.

Américo's father and oldest brother ran a dry goods store in downtown Brownsville on Washington Street. At the beginning of 1929, the economy was sound, and his older brother, Eliseo, borrowed money to invest in the store. Shortly afterwards, the October crash caused the bank to close. Paredes recalled that during the Great Depression, his family "had no money."[15]

He recalled that in the 1930s while delivering the Sunday morning edition of *The Brownsville Herald,* he encountered some *tequileros* (tequila smugglers) who frightened him. He had heard their bottles clanking as he delivered his newspapers in the early dawn. On one occasion when they saw him, they asked each other menacingly what to do with him. Paredes hoped that they were kidding, and he left. However, these individuals were probably not involved in organized gang activities. They just wanted liquor. Brownsville was a relatively quiet and peaceful town then.[16] For Paredes, Brownsville would remain a home of many memories. Although he left Brownsville in 1942, he returned to visit his relatives periodically. Years later, during the summers he would bring his family to visit border relatives and to enjoy South Padre Island. Paredes once said, "emotionally, it will always be my home town, but I recognize it less and less."[17] Many years later in the 1990s Paredes lamented that Brownsville had changed considerably because of the border drug trade.

It was also during these years that Paredes developed an interest in folktales and folk ballads. Until the age of fourteen, he and his twin brothers, Amador and Eleazar, spent their summers on their Uncle Vicente's ranch near Matamoros, which they preferred. The rest of the family went to San Antonio or South Padre Island to vacation. Paredes reminisced, "we would immediately head across the river the back way. Everyone had little boats hidden in the reeds. We would stay there three months living like Mexicans, listening to the old people tell their stories. My father would come down sometimes also, and at the end of August they would drive us back to Brownsville, and there I was living in another world."[18] That world, of course, was the world of ranchos, border tales about La Llorona, ballads about Juan Cortina, and Mexican traditions such as quinceañeras.

Paredes later dedicated the *Texas Mexican Cancionero: Folksongs of the Lower Border* to those individuals and to those times. Blanca Paredes, Américo's niece, said that she recalled Américo speaking about what happened on the rancho. The boys and men gathered mesquite wood in the afternoon for that evening's campfire. At night when the fire was lit, the old people sat, told stories, and sang ballads about the Mexican Revolution or folk heroes such as Jacinto Treviño or Gregorio Cortez. Sometimes they told jokes. Blanca remembers that Américo enjoyed the evenings immensely, perhaps not realizing that these experiences would later form the nucleus of his life's work.[19]

There were times when musicians from Matamoros visited Américo at his uncle Gualo's ranch on the outskirts of Brownsville. Paredes' nephew and long-time Brownsville educator, Manfred del Castillo, remembers that there was a musician named Ignacio Montelongo that Américo liked to listen to very much. "Nacho," as he was called, swam the river to sing corridos (folk ballads) or cantos (songs). At night the Manzano and the del Castillo families, both related to Uncle Gualo, listened to tales and songs of the border where their families had lived.[20] Those stories and that music entertained and instructed the young Américo and his relatives.

At the age of fourteen, Paredes had declared that he would work on the rancho in Mexico. After all, he had lived there during previous summers and thought that he could handle the work. He recalled how surprised he was,

> Of course, I was used to having everything done for
> me. I didn't even know how to saddle a horse. So the

horse did what they always do when you go to put the cinch; they fill themselves full of air and then you had to wait; so I did it and put my foot in. It was a gentle horse and I ended by the horses' feet... My father had a big laugh about it, and he said, "¿Y quieres ser ranchero?" [And you want to be a rancher?][21]

Paredes then decided to pursue other types of work.

Manfred del Castillo further remembers the days when he, Américo, and other boys stayed at his uncle's ranch. His comments provide a glimpse at the youthful Paredes that few people have ever seen.

My uncle had a ranch. He had 32 acres out there farmed up in cotton, tomatoes, watermelons... Américo enjoyed going out there. We used to go out there and spend some time. And every Saturday night, we would come to Brownsville in the truck con *los barandales*, [with the railings] in the truck and we would put everything in there, and we would come shopping, buy groceries and all that stuff and take it back. I was talking to Gualo a couple of nights ago, and he told me that one time that they were swimming in the river, and, of course, it was cold at the time, and they were on their little sandbar, and all of the sudden, one of the girls that was visiting *mi tía* Rafaelita came over to see, check on the boys, and they were, of course, all in their birthday suits... Américo was so embarrassed; he didn't want to get out of the water. He asked for his clothes, so they brought him his clothes, and he put his clothes on, and then he got out of the water with his clothes. And then on the way back, he rode on the fender of the car, and the wind, of course, was cold... He developed pneumonia, and he almost died. But he really did enjoy that because all of us enjoyed it. So those were the days

which were beautiful days. We had some good toma-
to fights out there, all the Manzanos and me. I was
just a younger kid. Of course they were older than I
was. They used to say "don't use any green ones; …
only use the overripe ones." Those were the ones we
could use. And also, the watermelons when we used
to go out there and pick the watermelons, and bring
them over and sell them in town. *Hay sandía colorada
y dulce* [there's watermelon, red and sweet], you know
and sell sandías, too. It was fun; it was really really
fun. Ride the horses, and then *desgranar elote* [shell
corn]; you know, oh man it was work, but it was fun
we would enjoy. He was a good man. Américo taught
Manfred's mother how to play the guitar. He really
enjoyed it because all of us enjoyed it. All we could
do was sing, play the guitar. There wasn't any other
entertainment whatsoever.[22]

Paredes' formative years in Brownsville and Matamoros were important to him. His strengthened ties with his family, his early education,
and the surrounding border environment all provided him with experiences that instructed and guided him for years to come.

CHAPTER TWO

THE DEPRESSION YEARS

When Américo was still attending junior high school, Blanca, one of his older sisters, died. He was both devastated and angry.

In 1931, Américo Paredes started high school at Brownsville High School. His experiences during those years were marked by both frustration and achievement. William Buford Beeson, one of Paredes' ninth grade classmates, had vivid recollections of Américo, whom he characterized as the brightest student he knew. He said that Américo was tall, slim, and light-complexioned and spoke very good English. They enrolled in English, mathematics, and Spanish classes. Beeson said that Américo was different. He was not too much involved in horseplay or fighting. He had a strong moral character and his teachers liked him because he was special.[23]

Américo, however, was also inquisitive, which at times produced negative consequences. He was strong willed and did not hesitate to challenge his teachers regarding content accuracy. To some instructors these questions exhibited little more than a lack of respect. To Américo they were legitimate requests for correct information.

Paredes said he had some problems with some teachers who had come from other states because teaching jobs were scarce. He received A's in all of his courses, except in a junior English course taught by Margaret Zachry. Paredes remarked, "She failed me because I wouldn't tell her I liked Walt Whitman. She gave me a book on Whitman and said it was great poetry. I said it was prose. I didn't understand it. She felt I had insulted her. I took junior English again and the principal told me just to apologize to her. Well, I apologized to her."[24]

The young Paredes eventually received a C in the course, but did not forget the incident. It was near the end of that junior year in 1933 that Paredes entered a poetry contest sponsored by Trinity College, located then in Waxahachie, Texas. When Paredes saw the announcement posted on the bulletin board, he completed the application and submitted a poem entitled "A Sonnet Tonight," which he later described as "forgettable." However, the poem won first prize. His high school principal, Mr. Irvine, was doubly impressed because Paredes won and because he took the initiative to enter the contest on his own. Américo learned about his award the following year when he was a senior. When Mrs. Zachry inquired about the prize that Paredes had received for winning, he replied that it was a leather-bound book from Spain. She then said that it was better than a "lousy" book of poetry. Many years later Paredes commented that those words told him what his teacher thought of poetry while she was teaching junior English.[25]

During his high school years, Paredes developed a serious interest in literature and music. The poetry contest gave him the confidence to pursue a career in writing, and as a junior he joined the staff of his high school yearbook. The editor was Reynaldo G. Garza, later appointed by President John F. Kennedy as the first Mexican American federal district judge. Garza recalled that Paredes helped him to complete the yearbook. Garza graduated that May and began his college studies in Austin two years later. Paredes contributed one essay, "The Tide," for the yearbook. It was about a scientist who conducted research near a fishing village and was swept out to sea by a storm. Although Paredes was only eighteen at the time he already had a grasp of the language and youthful creativity: "For a few seconds, it [the wave] held the ladder almost perpendicular. Its mighty hand played with it as a boy plays with straws. Then it fell backwards into the sea. The man did not cry out. He was past that."[26] The yearbook, called the *Palmegian*, was a hybrid of the high school yearbook, the *Palmetto,* and the junior college yearbook, the *Collegian.* It was created because of the prohibitive cost of producing two yearbooks during the hard times of the Great Depression, so one would serve both schools.

Paredes continued the learning process begun during his summers at his uncle's rancho. His mother sang ballads and told stories at home. His uncles and friends sang corridos around the rancho campfires near Matamoros. Américo enjoyed not only hearing stories, but also telling stories. His nephew Manfred del Castillo recalls:

> Américo would love to tell stories. And one night, we were all sitting in this two-story building where we used to sleep. It was next to our garage, and Américo was telling us a story about *La Llorona* or *el Monje Loco* [The Weeping Woman or the Crazy Monk]. I don't recall which one, but it was a real spooky story. He would get up and walk around and explain how the creatures looked with their teeth and their fiery eyes. He had a way of putting things that he kept you all in suspense… All of a sudden he walked over and turned off the light switch, and boy, pandemonium broke loose. Everybody started screaming, hollering, yelling, and running, and we jumped out the second story building. Some of them climbed out up to the garage, and others ran down the stairway… He was that type of person. He liked to play pranks on people, and we all laughed and we enjoyed things like that.[27]

The love of storytelling would remain with Américo throughout his life.

Paredes remembered an incident when he and his high school classmates stopped to say goodbye to an assistant principal after school. The assistant principal had a large paddle in his hand. When the young Paredes asked what the paddle was for, the man answered

"Para pegarles a los huercos" (to swat the kids). He had paddled some children for speaking Spanish.[28] Undoubtedly, those years would leave a lasting impression upon Américo Paredes.

As a senior in high school, Paredes had aspirations of attending college, but he could not afford it until a very opportune meeting with J. W. "Red" Irvine, the Brownsville High School principal and dean of the Brownsville Junior College. Paredes remembered,

> Well, school ends and I get my high school diploma. That was it; nowhere to go. I was standing on… a street in Brownsville with other kids, not looking for trouble, just standing around waiting for it to come around, I guess. But the dean and the principal drove by in a little Chevy with a rumble seat. And he saw me, stopped and backed up. It was late June and he called, and I went up and he said, "Are you going to college?" I said no I don't have the money. And he said, "did you apply for a student assistantship?" I told him, what's that.[29]

Irvine asked Paredes to complete a letter of application and said that he could secure an assistantship for him. It was arranged and Américo began to work twelve hours a week for Mrs. Pauline Good in exchange for the $150 semester tuition. Paredes did so well academically that he later became a member of Phi Theta Kappa, the junior college national honor society.

Even as a young man, Paredes enjoyed writing about what he knew best, the border. As a college freshman English student, he often wrote descriptive essays about the landscape he was familiar with and the culture in which he was raised. In "The Taste of the Habanero" he described the habanero pepper "as a wine although it is almost as strong as brandy…a taste resembling that of a piece of grapefruit rind that lingers in the palate."[30] In an essay entitled "The Evening" he described the huge clouds moving across the sky as *nubarrones*, a Spanish word that "conveys all the ponderous dignity of these enormous masses."[31] This essay received a grade of B with a teacher's comment at the top of page one indicating that Paredes should write more neatly.

One of his most memorable college essays captured a slice of saloon life in Matamoros, Tamaulipas, across the Río Grande from Brownsville. It was entitled "Afternoon in a Cantina."

> In the cantina, all is quiet. The bartender silently wipes one end of the bar with a cloth that once was white. At the other end, a pasty-faced boy leans, elbows on the bar, sipping dreamily a slender glass of beer. At a table sit three men. One, his head on the table, is asleep. Another is slumped in his chair, his head hanging back, his long Indian face blank, his mouth wide open. The last one, his fat face red and shiny, sways as he tries to bring a "schooner" of beer to his lips. At every attempt his hand shakes, and he spills some beer. With a petulant expression, he sets the glass down without tasting it. At the other table, a wrinkled man is dozing, a weather-beaten guitar in his horny fingers. No one speaks. Outside, the springs of an automobile complain of the streets of Matamoros.[32]

In the 1930s, the percentage of Spanish-surnamed residents in Brownsville was approximately 70 percent. However, the percentage attending Brownsville Junior College was probably less than 10 percent. Many Tejanos had dropped out of sight and many others could not afford to pursue college. Paredes recalled that he and a few of the Mexicano men that did attend became very good friends. They knew each other by nicknames. El Chaparro (The Short One) was Roberto Ramírez; Sabas Klahn, who was nearly six feet tall, was El Grandote (The Big One); and Paredes was El Flaco (The Thin One). He added, "You can look at me, and I'm still a flaco... We three were inseparable in college."[33] They remained friends for many years.

Paredes also remembered two or three of the Tejana students. One whom he got to know somewhat better was Berta Cabaza from

San Benito. He remembered that she was intelligent and collegial. She became a very good teacher there and eventually had a middle school named in her honor in San Benito, Texas.[34] Regrettably, Tejana students were a double minority. As women, access to college was limited to them and as Mexican Americans, many of their families did not encourage them or could not afford to pay for their education.

Shortly before Paredes completed his studies, his English teacher, Mrs. Hyman, asked everyone in the class what they were going to do after graduation. One student said that he would be attending the University of Colorado. Others planned to attend universities in Texas. She inquired about Américo's plans and he replied that he hoped to earn a Ph.D. in English at The University of Texas at Austin. She just looked at him and said, "Mr. Paredes, you have a facility with words. Why don't you try to get a job at the local newspaper?"[35] Although he felt hurt and insulted, she had told him the truth. How did Paredes expect to afford a university education? Paredes later realized that her statement was not intended to belittle him, but he did remember it for the rest of his life.

Ironically, Paredes did work for the local newspaper. First, however, he worked for Cárdenas and Sons, a grocery and general merchandise store. Américo drove one of two delivery trucks owned by Cipriano Cárdenas. He delivered items such as sugar and flour in large sacks or barrels. This was not an easy task for the thin Paredes, but he needed the work.

Paredes described the years from 1930 to 1936 as "years of transition from childhood to adult life, the unbalanced, blind years of metamorphosis."[36] During those years, he continued to write about what he knew and what he loved most: the border and its people. In 1936, however, turning points and changes were the norm for the twenty-one-year-old Paredes. In this year he not only finished writing his first poetry collections, "Black Roses" and "Cadencias," but also published his first poetry book, *Cantos de Adolescencia*. It was also during these years that he realized that his dreams of studying English at The University of Texas at Austin would have to be deferred.

"Cadencias," he described as a thing of itself, "a diary of the giddy days of adolescence—pitiful and laughable."[37] It is a Spanish collection that includes the translation of the *rimas* (poems) of Spanish poet Gustavo Adolfo Bécquer, whom he admired. In the foreword to "Black Roses," he wrote:

> Happy is he who has one tongue, one country, and one creed. His is a calm, even existence whose blessings he cannot realize. Consider the Mexico-Texan. He is the product of two countries that in the near past have been the bitterest of enemies—Mexico and Texas. Born of Mexican parents, he learns Spanish even as a bird learns to fly, his cradle is rocked by the sweet songs of the dark-eyed South; his childish mind is quickened by the folk-lore of Mexico and Spain; and his breast is stirred by tales of the prowess of his race.
>
> He goes to school and learns English. He learns the tinkling little songs of the Saxon child; he glories in Mother Goose; with Natty Bumpo, he explores the virgin wilderness; and he rides with Marion the Fox against the redcoats of King George.
>
> Thus he passes his early childhood, two persons in one, two individuals who as yet have not come to grips—a Mexican at home, an American at school. Then adolescence comes, and at this time, when he is no longer a child and not yet an adult, the Mexico-Texan realizes for the first time that he is neither Mexican or American... I have witnessed this struggle within myself.[38]

He overcame this struggle and many of his later writings empowered readers to learn about their history and be comfortable with their own identities.

"Las Golondrinas" ("The Swallows"), one of the initial poems in "Black Roses," first appeared in *The Valley Morning Star*, a Harlingen, Texas, newspaper, on November 18, 1934. Its title is the same as that of a popular Mexican song. This poem is about undying, unwavering love from one who has been left by another.

> Remember always in your misfortunes
> Though other passions may fade and wane
> That there is a soul that will stay beside you
> If your tomorrows,
> If your tomorrows,
> Are filled with pain.[39]

Cantos de Adolescencia was a significant work because it was his first published collection of poems. *Cantos* is divided into nine chapters beginning with "La Lira patriótica" (The Patriotic Lyre) and ending with "L'envoi" (verses concluding with a ballad which praise someone). Besides "Décimas" it includes sixty-one poems about love, rebellion, nature, and music. And although Paredes was later unhappy with the book, some of those original works reappeared years later in *Between Two Worlds*, published in 1991. According to Emilio Zamora, it is "a book of highly *nationalistic* poetry written in Spanish with entries from as early as the 1930s."[40] One poem in particular captures the essence of Paredes' first book of poetry. "A Mexico" embodies a passion and loyalty for the country that meant so much to him. Although he does not live there, his heart is always proud of it and if those in Mexico betray it, his heart quivers.[41] Paredes wrote,

> Yo te canté desde muy niño;
> amor por tu suelo muy joven sentí;
> mi primera poesía en nuestra lengua
> fué, patria, para ti.
>
> Yo te he visto por las páginas de historia
> caída y angustiada pero-no vencida!
> Has pasado por el crimen y la gloria:
> heróica, sacrosanta y fratricida.

Te baña con tu sangre el insurrecto,
te vende el estadista por dinero...
Conozco bien, mi patria, tus defectos
y porque los conozco, yo te quiero.

Cuando sé que das un paso hacía delante
mi corazón en tierra extraña se engrandece;
y si tus hijos te hieren por la espalda,
como si a él hirieran... se estremece.

To Mexico
(translation)

I sang of you since I was a child
A love for your soil I felt since very young
My first poem in our language
Was, my country, for you.

I have seen you in the pages of history
Fallen and anguished but not conquered!
Heroic, sacrosanct and fratricidal.

You are bathed by your blood of insurrection
The statesman sells you for money
I know well, my country, your defects
And because I know them, I love you.

When I know that you take one step forward
My heart on foreign soil swells with pride
And if your sons wound you in the back,
As if he were wounded—he trembles.[42]

Paredes later said, "my poetry in Spanish was protest because writing protest poetry wasn't so bad… A lot of it was horrible. I don't want to think about it anymore, but that's what I wanted to do."[43] Later in his life, Américo and some of his friends took all of the *Cantos* poetry books that he was able to find to the mouth of the Río Grande and burned them. Some, however, still exist. One was kept by his late brother, Lorenzo.

In the preface to *Cantos* he defines adolescence as a "physical phenomenon caused by the proximity of two ages; an individual who is neither child or adult." "These pages," he writes, "are the result of this struggle in the time of division."[44] The 1930s were indeed years of transition and challenges in his life. They were the growing years "desequilibrados de metamorfosis. En el tiempo en que se siente la primera pasión y la primera forma de amor patrio." (Imbalance in metamorphosis in the time when the first passion and the first form of love for country is felt.)[45] During these years, Paredes experienced romantic feelings for an Anglo high school classmate and a patriotic fervor for Mexico.

A second poem, "El Río Bravo," would reappear half a century later in English in *Between Two Worlds* as "The Río Grande." In this poem, twenty-one-year-old Américo describes the river, its path and currents, and his journey to join the river until it reaches its end. The poem is prophetic because after his death, Paredes would indeed be reunited with the river.

> The Río Grande
> Muddy river, muddy river,
> Moving slowly down your track
> With your swirls and counter-currents,
> As though wanting to turn back,
>
> As though wanting to turn back
> Towards the place where you were born,
> While your currents swirl and eddy,
> While you whisper, whimper, mourn;

So you wander down your channel
Always on, since it must be,
Till you die so very gently
By the margin of the sea.

All my pain and all my trouble
In your bosom let me hide,
Drain my soul of all its sorrow
As you drain the countryside,

For I was born beside your waters,
And since very young I knew
That my soul had hidden currents,
That my soul resembled you,

Troubled, dark, its bottom hidden
While its surface mocks the sun,
With its sighs and its rebellions,
Yet compelled to travel on.

When the soul must leave the body,
When the wasted flesh must die,
I shall trickle forth to join you,
In your bosom I shall die;

We shall wander through the country
Where your banks in green are clad,
Past the shanties of rancheros,
By the ruins of old Bagdad,

Till at last your dying waters,
Will release their hold on me,
And my soul will sleep forever
By the margin of the sea.[46]

One year before the publication of *Cantos,* Paredes was hired as a reporter for *The Brownsville Herald* and soon he published "The Mexico-Texan." This poem details what being born and growing up along the border meant to him. The first three verses describe his origins, his difficulty with the English language and the discrimination he is forced to endure.

> The Mexico-Texan he's one fonny man
> Who leeves in the region that's north of the Gran',
> Of Mexican father he born in these part,
> And sometimes he rues it dip down in he's heart.
>
> For the Mexico-Texan he no gotta lan',
> He stomped on the neck on both sides of the Gran',
> The dam gringo lingo he no cannot spik,
> It twisters the tong and it make you fill sick.
> A cit'zen of Texas they say that he ees,
> But then, why they call him the Mexican Grease?
> Soft talk and hard action, he can't understan',
> The Mexico-Texan he no gotta lan'.
>
> If he cross the reever, eet ees just as bad,
> On high poleeshed Spanish he break up his had,
> American customs those people no like,
> They hate that Miguel they should call him El Mike,
> And Mexican-born, why they jeer and they hoot,
> "Go back to the gringo! Go lick at hees boot!"
> In Texas he's Johnny, in Mexico Juan,
> But the Mexico-Texan he no gotta lan'.
>
> 1935[47]

Many of his early newspaper articles were about border folklore and traditions. In 1938 during the first Charro Days Celebration acknowledging the history and friendship between Brownsville and Matamoros, Paredes wrote about the celebration, bullfights, and *charreadas,* Mexican-style rodeos that emphasized horsemanship and roping skills. The articles were informative, accurate, and well-written. Many years later he commented that later writers for the *Herald* had reprinted and pirated some of his original pieces.[48] He also wrote freelance articles in English and Spanish for *El Regional,* a Matamoros newspaper, and *La Prensa,* the San Antonio daily. In *La Prensa,* Paredes wrote about the culture and traditions of the border in "Los Lunes Literarios" (The Literary Mondays), a section of the newspaper dedicated to literature. In Mercedes, Texas, one boy who read the articles and sold the newspapers was Rolando Hinojosa who later became a prominent Tejano writer.

During these early Charro Days events, Américo also became acquainted with the legendary conjunto pioneer, Narciso "Chicho" Martínez. Paredes had earlier attended some dances and quinceañeras at which Martínez performed and later they were booked at the same functions. Throughout the rest of their lives they continued to cross paths in the Valley and Austin.

Martínez, known as "El Huracán del Valle," was born in Reynosa, Tamaulipas, in 1911, and lived most of his life in La Paloma, near San Benito, Texas. In the mid-1930s he and his *bajo sexto* (twelve-string guitar) player, Santiago Almeida, began recording their *conjunto* (accordion/ guitar/ drum ensemble) music on the Bluebird Record label. In 1983 he received the prestigious National Endowment for the Arts award for lifelong achievement.[49] Paredes respected Martínez because of his talent and because he never let his fame "go to his head."[50] He referred to him as a virtuoso. Paredes once described Martínez in "Tres faces del pocho" this way,

> The scene is a little rundown 3.2 beer joint on the border los agachados. The bar is in the rear, facing front. Lights come up to the tune of a very fast polka played by Chicho Martínez (El Huracán del Valle) on a wheezy old accordion, accompanied by a bajo player who is obviously having trouble keeping up with Chicho.[51]

The irony is that Martínez never played in cantinas and that he would purchase a new accordion every six or seven months because he continuously wore them out.

Shortly after his retirement, Américo Paredes saw Narciso Martínez for the last time. Martínez had been booked to perform in Austin, and Paredes asked Chicho to stay at his home the night before. Martínez arrived tired after the long drive from the Río Grande Valley. They spoke briefly, and Chicho retired for the night. The next morning, Martínez served himself some coffee and, thinking no one could hear him, said "este café parece agua." (This coffee tastes like water.) Américo asked him if Nena, his wife, could make him more coffee. Martínez was surprised, embarrassed, and sheepishly said that it was fine. They laughed. When Martínez died of pulmonary complications on May 5, 1993, Paredes lost a genuine friend. [52]

From 1936 to 1939 Paredes also worked on his first novel, *George Washington Gómez,* which was eventually published in 1990 by Arte Público Press. He once said, "the introduction was misleading. It was in 1939 that this section was finished. The point is that I intended it to be volume one of a longer work and around 1939, when I was finishing this part, Hitler decided to invade Poland and the world changed and I had other things to do than writing. And I didn't come back to writing until I came in 1950 to Austin."[53] This five-part novel thinly disguises the Brownsville of his youth as Jonesville-on-the-Grande during the 1930s, a time of cultural conflict between Anglos and Tejanos along the South Texas border. Richard Bauman, author and former colleague of Paredes, describes this time and place as "a contact zone, a place shaped by the confluence—and conflict—of cultures and the struggle of identities."[54]

A sense of urgency was indeed evident as Paredes, although only twenty-three at the time, contemplated his life, his dreams and his inevitable death. In a collection of documents from 1938 titled "Old Notes," now held in the Paredes Papers at UT-Austin, the young Paredes showed a maturity beyond his years:

In my pockets, in my books, in the corners of my dust-covered desk are piles of little, folded scraps of paper with a few lines scribbled on each. They were to have been masterpieces, each and every one. Instead they lie like pieces of rusting machinery of a project that was begun but never finished. Sometimes I give myself a moment of time and I go through them, sorting them out, reading, examining. In many of them the idea, the essence, is gone forever. The words, hastily scribbled, are but bagasse from which the juice has been extracted. In others, the thought still lingers on faintly, like the perfume in a flower pressed for long between the pages of a book.

How I would like to sit down with these that still breathe life, and with the zeal of the doctor beside his dying patient, of the husbandman before a broken plant, nurse them slowly back to life - expanding, enlarging, perfecting, until they are what I first intended them to be.

It is this that makes me grieve. It is this that gives me a desperate feeling of futility and emptiness. For I know that I cannot revive them, that I cannot give to these dying thoughts the growth that will make them live. I am too preoccupied in other things, the result of which is the adding of more scraps of paper, more scraps of thought, in the pile that is covering me slowly.

For it has not been enough that myself be bifurcated by two languages and two cultures but that I must divide my energies into so many pursuits that I can master none. I am like the leader who, drunk by initial victories, tries to effect a multitude of rich conquests simultaneously, dividing his forces into so many fields of battle that they barely stand their ground against the opposing hordes. And the leader, confident in his superiority and ability—poor fool— unwilling to lose a single of his intended conquests, finds himself loath to recall his forces so that he may reorganize them and have a hope of victory. Instead, he keeps them in the field, though inwardly he fears the inevitable defeat in every sector.

So hopelessly disorganized and scattered, my aspirations, though not in full flight, find themselves unable to advance, and that is paramount to defeat. I feel the world rushing past, and I am standing still. The harness that ties me to the responsibilities of life irks me like a close and enveloping thing. It chafes me so that I would gladly throw it to the winds and race wildly against the world if I but dared. But I do not dare.

And the seconds tick away into hours, the hours into years. Time glides by like a fox, scarcely seeming to move, yet traveling at a lightning pace. And I am standing still. Each minute throws a silk-like thread around me, tying me down more firmly to the place where, Gulliver-like, I sprawl. It is futile that I strain at my bonds, so tenuous yet so strong. It is useless that I fret against the inevitable.[55]

Paredes' sense of despair can be seen as typical of many people during this time. The Great Depression has been called a numbing experience for the millions who lived through it. Its impact was devastating and caused mass unemployment, bank closings, foreclosures of mortgages, and a general economic panic.[56] Paredes managed to survive working at several jobs, but working so hard just to survive probably frustrated his attempts at a more intellectual and creative career as a writer and musician. In addition to working at La Perla Bakery he also worked at the newspaper for a salary of $11.40 weekly. One of the sons of Cipriano Cárdenas, the former employer of Paredes, sponsored a weekly fifteen-minute program at radio station KWWG. Paredes sang his songs and played his guitar for what he said was "the magnificent sum of a dollar a minute fifteen minutes a week."[57] In 1940, he began to work at a third job at Pan American Airways, which was participating in the American war preparedness program shortly after World War II had begun in Europe. He earned approximately twenty dollars a week. He later said that it "was pretty good money back then."[58] However, Paredes was furious when he discovered that he was getting paid less than an Anglo doing the same work.

> I worked side by side with an Anglo about my age and with the same amount of education. We had the same job, the same rating. Then one day, in conversation, he happened to mention his salary. He was making $100 a month, doing the same job I did for $65. I asked my immediate superior about it, and he was quite frank with me. "Of course he makes more than you," he said. "But that is because he just couldn't live on $65 a month. You can."
>
> As you can see, my boss did believe the young Anglo and I were *physically* different. He must have thought my stomach was constructed differently, so I could thrive on cheap food, while the Anglo couldn't, much like goats, who are said to thrive on poor pasturage, or even tin cans, while other animals—say thoroughbred horses—required finer food.[59]

It was during one of his radio performances that Paredes met Consuelo "Chelo" Silva, who was seven years younger than he. Chelo was born on August 25, 1922, in Brownsville. She was one of seven children and her mother, Margarita, washed and ironed clothes for affluent families to support her children. From a young age, Chelo had displayed a unique singing ability. When she was eleven, she sang in the Guadalupe Catholic Church choir. Her voice had such resonance that people began to ask her mother if she could perform at their fiestas and *kermesas*, which were church-related festivals. She would give her permission to sing as long as she could accompany her. By her mid-teens, Chelo was performing throughout the Brownsville area and had acquired a reputation for her deep powerful voice. By her late teens, she was singing with the Tito Crixell Orchestra at various religious and social functions in Brownsville, as well as on the radio, when she met Américo.

Shortly after they first met, Américo began to court Consuelo. Soon they performed together on a radio program with Chelo singing and Américo accompanying her on the guitar. In 1938, they performed their music at the El Jardín Hotel during the first Charro Days Celebration. During that same year, Chelo sang the first Charro Days song, "La Fiesta Charra," written by Tito Crixell.

The Paredes family did not accept Silva or her emerging singing career, but Américo and Chelo married anyway on August 13, 1939. Angélica, Chelo's younger sister, described the couple as supporters of each other's emerging artistic careers. Chelo accompanied Américo to his fiestas and Américo accompanied her to her quinceañeras.[60]

Emilio Zamora, Associate Professor at The University of Texas at Austin, writes that during their brief marriage, they lived a Bohemian lifestyle, socializing with musicians, artists, writers, and poets on both sides of the border. [61] Some in Brownsville old enough to remember them said that they were an ideal couple. Chelo was young, attractive, and a popular singer. Américo was handsome, confident, a talented writer, and musician.[62] However, both had strong personalities and both were determined to have successful careers. In 1942, Américo Jr., their only child, was born. Five years later, they divorced, probably victims of their individual success and time spent apart. Chelo's sister, Angélica, recalled that the divorce hurt Chelo because "I guess she really cared for him." For a time, Chelo worked at the E. Manatou clothing store and J.C. Penney in downtown Brownsville. She recorded her first record at the age of twenty. Then her recording career skyrocketed and by the 1950s she was known as "La Reina del Bolero" (The

Bolero Queen). She often sang about deceit, adversity, heartbreak, and a lack of inhibition. "La Historia de Un Amor" (The History of One Love), "Me Tengo que Matar" (I Must Kill Myself), "Inolvidable" (Unforgettable) and "Como un Perro" (Like a Dog) were some of her well-known songs. Although she did not record many ranchera songs, one, "Pregúntame a Mi" (Ask Me) is memorable. Its lyrics state that she has gone astray because she loved the wrong man. She drinks to forget him and drinks even more to be absolutely sure that she will not remember him. Chelo Silva soon became the best-selling artist on both sides of the lower U.S./Mexico border.[63] In McAllen, Texas, she recorded for Falcón Records. In Mexico City, Chelo recorded for the Columbia and Sony companies.

Silva also toured extensively in Mexico, performing in cities such as Guadalajara, Monterrey, Juárez, and Mexico City and often accompanying entertainers such as José Alfredo Jiménez and Lola Beltrán. In the United States she performed throughout Texas, in Arizona, California, Illinois, and on the East Coast. Silva also toured with the Javier Cugat Orchestra.

Américo and Chelo divorced on September 6, 1947, when Américo Jr. was four years old. "Ameriquito," as he was called, remained with his mother. Although Américo Sr. disliked the idea of Chelo recording and touring and being away from their son, this was how she earned her living. Américo Jr. lived with his grandparents and aunts while his mother was on the road.

Although no longer living with him, Américo Jr. was quite proud of his famous father. When he was attending Brownsville High School, his teacher asked the students where their fathers worked. He replied that his father worked at The University of Texas at Austin. The teacher in disbelief asked if his father worked in the maintenance department. Américo Jr. replied that his father was a professor there, and his Uncle Amador later verified it because the teacher would not believe it.

Chelo Silva remarried in the later 1940s. She and her husband, Leopoldo Pérez, lived in Corpus Christi, Texas, for the rest of their lives. They had three children. In the mid-1980s, Chelo contracted stomach cancer, and after four painful years of the disease, died on April 2, 1988.[64]

Chelo, although controversial at times with her suggestive lyrics and her reputation for excessive drinking, nevertheless will be remembered. Silva's music entertained a generation of *frontereños* (border people), and a new generation of Chicana and Chicano scholars are investigating her historical and musical contributions.[65] Her legacy to Paredes was in accompanying him during those early years as an emerging writer and musician, his last years in Brownsville, and in bearing their son, Américo Jr., who went on to serve in the Air Force for many years until he retired.

World War II changed Américo's life dramatically. He joined the military despite the exemption from the draft that his work at Pan American Airways afforded him. He later wrote about this pivotal decision, "I shall never cease to bless the day that I decided to quit PAA. That was the cutting of the rope that kept me riding at anchor in prejudice, smugness, and general littleness of soul and mind."[66] Two of his friends, Miguel Morán and Matías Serrata, also joined up and lost their lives in the war. Morán was involved in an accident on the island of Attu. He returned home and died. Serrata landed in France and never returned.

In a few short years Paredes went from high school student, to aspiring musician and writer, to family man. Yet it was his decision to join the army that forever changed his life.

CHAPTER THREE

THE WAR AND POST-WAR YEARS

Paredes commented about how he entered the military. His experience as a reporter was probably the deciding factor.

> I could not volunteer because at that time this
> was in '44 already. They did not want people in the
> Navy; they did not want people in the Air Force. They
> wanted people with rifles. They weren't called grunts
> at that time, but that is what they wanted. So they told
> me "go home; we'll call you." I worked for the *Herald*
> for a time. And they took me. In a way it was very
> good for me because someone who had been reading
> too many detective books saw that I was a newspaper
> reporter and they put me in the CID, the Criminal
> Investigation Division. Now they were supposed to be
> detectives.

> There was one other reporter from California. All
> the rest were former highway patrolmen, detectives,
> and we were supposed to be trained in law enforcement... Of course, I washed out in that so they sent
> me to Seattle, and at the time the war ended anyway.
> So by the time I ended up in Japan, the war was over.
> Again, a lucky break... they were starting a newspaper
> at the base... and these people went to see whom they
> could pick to work in the paper... And the group—
> they were all people with a college education, two

from New York and San Francisco, both from Jewish extraction, both left wing radicals *hasta las cachas* [to the hilt] and one was a member of the Communist Party.[67]

They had read Hart Stilwell's book, *Border City*, narrated by a cynical reporter from Brownsville who wrote about race relations. Although born in Yoakum, Texas, Stilwell lived in the Río Grande Valley until he enrolled at The University of Texas at Austin at age seventeen. His father was a Texas Ranger.[68] Paredes said, "they asked me if I had heard of the book and I replied that I was in it."[69] Stilwell had earlier read and edited Paredes' own manuscript, probably *George Washington Gómez*. That convinced the CID to hire Paredes and he worked in Tokyo until 1946. Paredes admitted that his experiences there "broadened my horizons."[70]

As a result, Paredes wrote and edited articles in *The G Eye Opener*, a military newsletter. The Paredes sense of humor was evident in many of these articles. One particular article entitled "Chaplain Dalton Won't Get Cold Feet" reads as follows:

> Every soldier dreams of having someone care for his welfare. Our friend Chaplain Dalton is one up on all of us. He has a friend who does not let him get cold feet. This friend after learning that it was necessary a visitor remove his shoes in a Japanese house, sent the chaplin a fine pair of pink knitted booties, his one Christmas present. At all future sukiyaki dinners the chaplain will be a sensation.[71]

Then Paredes began writing and serving as political editor for the Tokyo-based *Pacific Stars and Stripes*, the Armed Forces daily newspaper. His primary topics were the aftermath of the war and the Japanese war trials. His themes were varied including a plot to assassinate Douglas MacArthur, the riots and storming of Premier Shidehara's home, and widespread hunger in Tokyo. One particular article published on May 2, 1946, was entitled "Half Million Japanese Parade in Tokyo Streets in May Day Celebration." It was about Japanese protesters against the emperor who read a message to General Mac-Arthur thanking him for the U.S. government resistance against the new Japanese government that sent officials to supervise food rationing for the Japanese people.[72]

In 1946, he was discharged but remained in the Far East for four more years. He then began to work in public relations for the International Branch of the American Red Cross. He traveled in China for one year and later in Korea, Manchuria, and Japan. These travels would later be chronicled in his poetry. About Korea, he wrote,

> Korea
> When the falling snow
> Had covered the old plum tree
> We dreamed of the spring,
> Now I am alone
> Under the falling blossoms
> Of the sakura.
>
> —
>
> Because
> Tears are such a waste
> Pain comes a little harder
> Than for most to you and me,
> Ours is a smiling
> And a frugal people.
>
> —
>
> The face
> Of the Chosen people
> Is the face of a baby
> That has lived ten thousand years,
> That is why their flag
> Is red and blue.[73]

José Limón would later comment about Paredes' stay in the Far East after the war:

> Here's a fellow who's in the second world war and
> winds up in Japan and any commonsensical reaction

to that world war experience and having been there would immediately call for the average soldier to come right back home. Instead, he chooses to stay and almost as if he were producing an exiledom as it were. We are all familiar with African American exiles to Paris, but have you ever heard of a Mexican who exiles to the East, a form of exile, not to return home for several years. And then there is a question of the imagined community. I have the sense that he wished to have no imagined community, the intellectual world citizen, the cosmopolitan. It is a figure that a lot of us are going to struggle against because we spend so much time in thinking of Américo Paredes as our own… a leader in our nation.[74]

While working in Shanghai in March 1947, Paredes wrote a letter to his brother Eliseo. In it he commented about how difficult it was to find Spanish language books, but finally finding one Spanish-Japanese second-hand dictionary. Paredes also included a verse he had written in 1937 about the Spanish and their New World conquest, which read,

Raza gloriosa y real de mis abuelos
O mi raza giganta
que aplastaste el polvo con tu planta
cuanto guerrero altivo,
que cruzaste los montes y los mares
llevando dondequiera tus altares
y en tu lenguaje dulce y expresivo
el oro vivo.

Glorious and genuine race of my grandparents
O my gigantic race
That you crushed into dust with your heel
Many a proven warriors
Who crossed forests and oceans

> Taking your altars everywhere
> And in your sweet and expressive language
> The living gold.[75]

In 1947 and 1948, Américo wrote a weekly column for *El Universal*, a prominent Mexico City newspaper. His articles focused primarily on post-war Asia and his experiences there. Hunger, corruption, and the rebuilding of war-torn countries were often detailed in his writing.

It was in Japan that Paredes met the woman who would be his love and partner for life, Amelia "Nena" Sidzu Nagamine. Amelia was the daughter of a Japanese diplomat and a Uruguayan mother. She was born on October 31, 1921, in Montevideo, Uruguay. Soon after, her parents moved to Buenos Aires, Argentina, where she grew up, before eventually moving to Japan. Before they had been formally introduced, Amelia had heard someone speaking Spanish on a bus. It was Américo Paredes. The two were formally introduced by Jerry Davis, a mutal friend who believed that since the two knew Spanish, they might enjoy speaking it to each other. Américo wrote at the time,

> Then—October 13, 1947—my life changed radically. Visiting the ARC Ginza-offices, Jerry Davis introduced me to Amelia—and things soon came to a head. By Oct. 31 I was smitten, by November 11 I had told her I loved her, by Nov. 13 we had decided to marry. Here was what I had dreamed about, and in spite of all my comments on women, I fell—for good. We understand each other. She will be my guide, my Pole star through life. Perhaps so it may be realized—not blending flashes of pain—but open-eyed tenderness. Something of the "romanticism" of my life has gone out—but something new and better has taken its place. There never was anything in my life like this. Our sweet and bitter moments of courtship do not belong here. Neither do the problems that arose over

our past... We met those problems and conquered them. At last, at long last, there is a measure of peace and purpose within my tender, melancholy segment of my life—goodbye, perhaps forever. May this new one be fruitful and may it be long.[76]

He was correct. They wed on May 28, 1948, and remained married for over fifty years.

Fifty years later they comically recalled about how they fell in love. Américo remembered, "One day I was working for the American Red Cross and had just finished arranging some boxes. As I was leaving I saw this girl I had seen before and said, 'adiós.' She then said, 'Adiós, Ameriquito.' I was like a fish. She had cast out the line and I was hooked. She was reeling me in."[77] Amelia had a different version of that meeting, saying that if she had known what she had at the end of the line, she would have thrown it back. For a moment they both laughed, reminisced, and reflected briefly on five decades of marriage.

Throughout their marriage, the couple used their given names publicly and at times Amelia used her nickname Nena. However, privately and in some of their early correspondence, they used the names of "Gusai" (Amelia) and "Dana" for Américo. These names were very personal and represented a private affection for each another.[78]

During his time in Asia until 1950, Américo traveled repeatedly throughout the area. Their correspondence during this time reveals how difficult it was for them to be apart and how much they loved each other. In a letter he wrote while in Seoul, Korea, before they married, Américo reiterated how she had changed his life.

Tenía tanto tiempo de haber dejado de importarme del futuro y de mi propio mejoramiento. Pasaba por la vida como la cigarra, cantando, sin pensar en el frío atardercer. Ahora todo mi mundo ha cambiado y ha cambiado porque lo has cambiado tú. Mi vida era tierra estéril donde la semilla de mis sueños dormía en los zurcos. Llegó tu amor, me sacudió con tus tormentas y me sonrió con tus soles, y el campo floreció. No puedo escribir más; no le puedo decir a esta maquina más veces que te quiero... Contéstame; piensa mucho en mí; quiéreme más que nunca. Y hasta que vuelva de este destierro me consolaré con los recuerdos.

Te quiero,
Américo

It's been so long since the future and my proper betterment mattered to me. I passed through life like a locust, singing, without thinking of the cold late afternoon. Now all my world has changed and it has changed because you have changed it. My life was barren soil where the seed of my dreams slept in the rows. Your love arrived; it shook me with its storms and I smiled with your sunshine and the fields bloomed. I cannot write more; I cannot tell this machine any more that I love you... Answer me; think much about me; love me more than ever. And until I return from this journey, I will console myself with memories.

I love you,
Américo [79]

Few events affected the life of Américo Paredes as much as World War II. Not only did he travel through much of the Orient and marry the woman of his dreams, but his experiences working with the *The G Eye Opener* and the *Pacific Stars and Stripes* afforded him opportunities to continue writing. He remained in the Far East for four years after World War II, but by 1950 was ready to return to the States with a new bride and his goal of completing his education.

CHAPTER FOUR

PURSUING A DREAM

During his time in Asia, Américo had taken correspondence courses in the Armed Forces through a program called USAFI (U. S. Armed Forces Institute) adding more to his college hours. He recalled, "I realized I didn't want to go back to Brownsville with just a Junior College education... There wasn't anything for me to do that I would want to do."[80] Paredes returned to Brownsville for a visit in 1950 a changed man. He wrote, "returning as I did in January to the becalmed anchorage. The old harbor resented the new shape of my sails. Klahn as well called me a snob and a pretender because I told him I have found beauties not only in free verse but in symphonic music and modern art. What a fool I was until I cast anchor... That I can see plainly now—after my trip home—My past was mirrored in the present of my old ex-friends."[81] The combination of these correspondence courses and previous college courses at Brownsville Junior College laid the foundation for further studies. However, the couple now faced a new challenge. They were informed at the consulate in Yokohama that because Amelia was from Japan, she could not live in the United States. At that time other Asians were allowed to immigrate, but not the Japanese. She was required to apply for a six-month visa with a stipulation that she violate no laws. Compliance would permit her to receive another six-month visa after which she would be allowed to immigrate. Meanwhile, her year would be spent in Matamoros, and once again the couple was apart.[82] Lorenzo, Américo's older brother, remembered that trying time,

I helped him when he came back from Japan. They would not let his wife into the country, so she stayed in Mexico at Eliseo's house. I took Américo to Austin; his wife stayed in Matamoros. Américo would call me, and I would bring him to Brownsville from Austin. Then, he would go to Matamoros to visit his wife and take care of some paperwork. I would also take him back to Austin. That is how I helped him. I would go back and forth.[83]

It was a difficult time, but Américo periodically visited Nena while working on his bachelor of arts in English and Spanish at The University of Texas. Within a year, he completed his first degree, earning the highest academic honors, *summa cum laude*. That same year, Nena moved to Austin to join him and he began to work on his masters. Paredes became a graduate teaching fellow teaching English and gaining valuable experience in the classroom. Like many other married graduate students, Américo faced academic and economic challenges. Although he was almost middle-aged, Paredes had not forgotten his dream of earning a Ph.D. from The University of Texas. He remembered,

Well, the fact is this had been my ambition and I know that time was running out. I mean you don't know there are people coming back to school. At 35 you're middle aged. I was sitting in that first year, I was sitting with young kids, but after that I went into graduate school; of course, and it was different. I wanted to get it and I wanted to give our side. But I think if I had not had those two years of junior college, courtesy of Red Irvine, I would not have had the guts, if I may say, to come back at the age of thirty five.[84]

Also important to note is that his self-titled "dead years" had ended. Paredes now embarked on the academic journey that would result in his doctorate and gain him future national recognition as a folklorist and scholar.

One of Américo's graduate school classmates, Delbert Runyon, a long-time Spanish instructor at The University of Texas at Brownsville and son of nationally known photographer Robert Runyon, fondly remembered Paredes. Runyon was already a graduate student when Paredes returned from the Far East and enrolled for classes. They enrolled in three of the same classes: Chaucer, Literary Criticism, and Literature of the Southwest. Runyon commented about Paredes: "He was a very quiet person. He studied hard... he did very well."[85]

Runyon recalled that Paredes once came to him for advice. He had won a writing contest and had received a thousand dollars specifically for the purchase of books. Américo lived in a damp World War II barrack apartment and his books began to mildew. Runyon suggested that he take them out in the sun for awhile. He also remembered going to a private bookstore called the Bookstall near the university and seeing J. Frank Dobie buying books. Runyon was complimentary about Paredes and their time at The University of Texas at Austin. He ended by saying "What else can I say? It was a pleasant relationship."[86]

In 1956, Paredes completed his doctorate in English, folkore, and Spanish. He said that he "worked like hell and let my wife run the house and everything while I worked to get two degrees."[87] In doing so, Paredes became the first Mexican American to receive a Ph.D. in English from The University of Texas at Austin. He had completed a lifelong goal and had opened the doors for others to enter.

His thesis was both groundbreaking and controversial. His topic was a ballad about Gregorio Cortez, a Texas Mexican folk hero, who lived at the turn of the twentieth century. Paredes first heard the ballad sung by his mother and by the old men on the ranchos along the river. The men glorified Cortez, who managed a heroic escape from the Texas Rangers. Paredes made a decision to find the truth about the controversial character. He commented,

> I was very much aware... I was not the only one who
> believed that what we were taught in school at the

time and what we knew in our hearts and what our
parents told us was different; that our heritage was
not being given the respect that it deserved. The
thing was that most of what people knew were in corridos, in legends and in oral history. And I wanted to
bring these things to the majority.[88]

He would do this for the next four decades.

Paredes dedicated the book to his father and to the old men who
had taught him so much: "To the memory of my father, who rode a
raid or two with Catarino Garza; and to all those old men who sat
around on summer nights, in the days when there was a chaparral,
smoking their cornhusk cigarettes and talking in low, gentle voices
about violent things; while I listened."[89]

Paredes was meticulous in his research. He examined court records and interviewed those who had known Cortez, including his
son, Valeriano. Paredes was most grateful to the Cortez family for
providing him the necessary information. In one letter to Louis Cortez, the grandson of Gregorio Cortez, Paredes thanked him and his
father for loaning him a text of the corrido. He also told the son
that his father had mentioned some photographs and that he would
appreciate borrowing them.[90] From this data, Paredes reconstructed
the tragic story of Gregorio Cortez.

Cortez was born on June 22, 1875, on a border rancho between
Matamoros and Reynosa in Tamaulipas, Mexico.[91] He and his brother Romualdo were farming a piece of rented land near Kenedy in
Karnes County, Texas, when Sheriff Morris and two deputies rode
to the place in pursuit of a horse thief. Since the sheriff spoke no
Spanish, he relied on one of his deputies for translation. The translator was not sufficiently proficient in Spanish either, and because of
a translation error involving the Spanish word for *mare*, the sheriff
tried to arrest Cortez and shot his brother. Cortez then shot and
killed the sheriff in self-defense and fled, knowing that he would not
get a fair trial in that region of Texas.[92] For ten days, hundreds of
men, including sheriffs, deputies, Texas Rangers, and posses, looked

for him. No one could capture him until Jesús González, alias El Teco (a shortened version of "tecolote," meaning owl), betrayed him. Paredes explains that during the chase, Cortez "walked at least one hundred twenty miles and rode more than four hundred on … brown… and sorrel mares." Cortez repeatedly crossed back and forth over the same area to confuse those who were after him, some of whom were convinced that he was the head of an entire gang.[93]

Gregorio Cortez became a folk hero for Texas Mexicans. Both the legend and the ballad of Cortez emphasized that the Anglo Americans were able to capture him only because he decided to give himself up to spare his people further suffering. Some versions of the incident contend that every man who offered Cortez water was severely beaten and thrown in jail. Other Mexicans who fed him were hanged because they had refused to reveal the direction Cortez was going. Although some of the details described in the ballad and the legend are embellishments, Paredes' research revealed that indeed many Mexicans were victimized because of the Cortez incident. The Anglo American authorities harassed Cortez's mother, wife, and children and put them in jail. In addition, a friend who had helped him, the friend's wife, and their children were also jailed; in some cases they had received gunshot wounds. The most blatant example of such mistreatment was the case of a thirteen-year-old Mexican boy, accused of being a member of the nonexistent Cortez gang, who was nearly fatally hanged from a tree.[94]

In his introduction to his dissertation, Paredes explained that his book was an examination of a ballad and the story of a ballad hero. It was a border Mexican narrative folksong, a corrido about a man "who defended his right with his pistol in his hand."[95] What follows is one of several variants that Américo Paredes collected.

> Gregorio Cortez
> En el condado de El Carmen
> miren lo que ha sucedido,
> murió el Cherife Mayor,
> quedando Román herido.

Serían las dos de la tarde
cuando la gente llegó;
unos a otros dicen:
No saben quien lo mató.

Se anduvieron informando
como media hora despúes
supieron que el malhechor
era Gregorio Cortez.

Ya insortaron a Cortez
por toditito el estado,
que vivo o muerto se aprehenda
porque a varios ha matado.

Decía Gregorio Cortez
con su pistola en la mano:
- No siento haberlo matado,
lo que siento es a mi hermano. –

Decía Gregorio Cortez
con su alma muy encendida:
- No siento haberlo matado,
la defensa es permitida. –

Venían los americanos
más blancos que una amapola,
de miedo que le tenían
a Cortez con su pistola.

Decían los americanos,
decían con timidez:
- Vamos a seguir la huella
que el malhechor es Cortez. -

Soltaron los perros jaunes
pa' que siguieran la huella,
pero alcanzar a Cortez
era seguir a una estrella.

Le echaron los perros juanes
pa' que siguieran la huella,
pero alcanzar a Cortez
era seguir a una estrella.

Tiró con rumbo a Gonzales
sin ninguna timidez:
- Síganme, rinches cobardes,
yo soy Gregorio Cortez. -

Se fue de Belmont al rancho,
lo alcanzaron a rodear,
poquitos más de trescientos,
y allí les brincó el corral.

Cuando les brincó el corral,
según lo que aquí se dice,
se agarraron a balazos
y les mató otro cherife.

Decía Gregorio Cortez
con su pistola en la mano:
- No corran, rinches cobardes,
con un solo mexicano. -

Decía Gregorio Cortez
les gritaba en alta voz :
- Mis armas no las entrego
hasta estar en calaboz'. –

Decía Gregorio Cortez,
decía en su voz divina :
- Mis armas no las entrego
hasta estar en bartolina. –

Ya agarraron a Cortez
ya terminó la cuestión,
la pobre de su familia
lo lleva en el corazón.

Ya con esto me despido
a la sombra de un ciprés,
aquí se acaba cantando
el corrido de Cortez.

Gregorio Cortez (translation). Note: The English
translation contains extra verses consistent with different versions of the ballad that circulated, thus
making it longer than the Spanish version.

In the county of El Carmen, look what has
    happened;
the Major Sheriff is dead, leaving Román badly
    wounded.

In the county of El Carmen such a tragedy took
    place:
the Major Sheriff is dead; no one knows who killed
    him.

They went around asking questions about half an
    hour afterward;
they found out that the wrongdoer had been Grego-
    rio Cortez.

Now they have outlawed Cortez throughout the
      whole of the state;
let him be taken, dead or alive, for he has killed sev-
      eral men.

Then said Gregorio Cortez, with his pistol in his
      hand,
"I don't regret having killed him; what I regret is my
      brother's death."

Then said Gregorio Cortez, with his soul aflame,
"I don't regret having killed him; self-defense is
      permitted."

The Americans were coming; they were whiter than
      a poppy
from the fear that they had of Cortez and his pistol.

Then the Americans said, and they said it fearfully,
"Come, let us follow the trail, for the wrongdoer is
      Cortez."

They let loose the bloodhounds so they could follow
      the trail,
but trying to overtake Cortez was like following a
      star.

He struck out for González, without showing any
      fear:
"Follow me, cowardly rinches; I am Gregorio
      Cortez."

From Belmont he went to the ranch, where they suc-
      ceeded in surrounding him,

quite a few more than three hundred, but he
    jumped out of their corral.

When he jumped out of their corral, according to
    what is said here,
they got into a gunfight, and he killed them another
    sheriff.

Then said Gregorio Cortez, with his pistol in his
    hand,
"Don't run, you cowardly rinches, from a single
    Mexican."

Gregorio Cortez went out, he went out toward
    Laredo;
they would not follow him because they were afraid
    of him.

Then said Gregorio Cortez, "What is the use of your
    scheming?
You cannot reach me, even with those
    bloodhounds."

Then said the Americans, "If we catch up with him,
    what shall we do?
If we fight him man to man, very few of us will
    return."

Way over near El Encinal, according to what is said
    here,
they made him a corral, and he killed them another
    sheriff.

Then said Gregorio Cortez, shooting out a lot of
    bullets,
"I have weathered thunderstorms; this little mist
    doesn't bother me."

Now he has met a Mexican, he says to him haughtily,
"Tell me the news; I am Gregorio Cortez."

"They say that because of me many people have
    been killed;
so now I will surrender, because such things are not
    right."

Cortez said to Jesús, "At last you are going to see it;
go and tell the rinches that they can come and ar-
    rest me."

All the rinches were coming, so fast that they almost
    flew,
because they were going to get the ten thousand
    dollars that were offered.

When they surrounded the house, Cortez appeared
    before them:
"You will take me if I'm willing but not any other
    way."

Then said the Major Sheriff, as if he was going to
    cry,
"Cortez, hand over your weapons; we do not want to
    kill you."

Then said Gregorio Cortez, shouting to them in a
     loud voice,
"I won't surrender my weapons until I am in a cell."

Then said Gregorio Cortez, speaking in his godlike
     voice,
"I won't surrender my weapons until I'm inside a
     jail."

Now they have taken Cortez, and now the matter is
     ended;
his poor family are keeping him in their hearts.

Now with this I say farewell in the shade of a cypress;
this is the end of the ballad of Don Gregorio
     Cortez.[96]

The Paredes dissertation faced several obstacles before being approved by the English Department. The first was that it was a work about a Texas Mexican whose corrido was originally written in Spanish, not English. A second obstacle was that it criticized, among others, folklorist Walter Prescott Webb and the Texas Rangers. Although his dissertation committee had comments and reservations about portions of the work, the committee members were willing to accept it. Paredes had been accurate and meticulous in his research. He said, "It happened that my dissertation was written in the English Department. It is a strange thing too because it is about a Mexican hero, a ballad in Spanish, and much of my research was done in Spanish, yet, they accepted it."[97]

Their approval was also helped by the encouragement of Stith Thompson. Thompson, head of the folklore program at Indiana University, visited The University of Texas at Austin. Thompson had begun his career at Austin and had taught in the English Department. In 1955, he was invited to return as a visiting professor. He arrived shortly before the committee approved the dissertation and told the committee that he was going to tell The University of Texas Press to publish it. Paredes believed that Thompson had influenced the process. He referred to Thompson as "Mr. Folklore" in the United States and Europe. Paredes said, "this was almost like the supreme being, *un dedazo* [a divine appointment], so the Press accepted it."[98] He championed Paredes' work on a campus that had not been known for its enthusiasm toward Mexican American scholars or students.

After graduation, Paredes found it difficult to find employment in Austin. He then applied for and accepted a teaching position in the English Department at Texas School of Mines (later The University of Texas at El Paso) in 1957. He taught there for a year and prepared his dissertation for publication.

While teaching in El Paso, Américo was contacted by The University of Texas Press. The director, Frank W. Wardlaw, said that he liked the manuscript, but that some changes would have to be made. Most of the changes targeted comments made about J. Frank Dobie, Walter Prescott Webb, and the Texas Rangers, in addition to suggesting that the manuscript be shortened by one-fourth to one-third. Wardlaw made the following comments about the book.

> Upon going over your dissertation again, I find myself less confident about what should be done with it than I was several months ago. The dissertation is a brilliant job and is quite worthy of publication as it stands. However, its present form limits its appeal to a few hundred professional folklorists. We believe that reorganization can extend its appeal to general readers in the thousands.
>
> There are several main elements in this work which are of great value and interest to the general reader. One of these is your exceedingly penetrating analysis of the border country and its people. Another, and this may be the most important contribution of all, lies in your analysis of the Texas legend which

has grown up about the Mexican people and about the Texas Rangers. Dr. Walter Prescott Webb, who is chairman of the faculty advisory board, says that this particular service is long overdue, although he ruefully finds himself the villain of the piece at several points. He says that he has always considered it a weakness of his book on the Texas Rangers that he was unable to give the Mexican attitude toward the Rangers, and their side of the border conflict, with any degree of thoroughness. He says that he made an effort to get this material but was unable to do so largely because of the language barrier. Your presentation of the Mexican side of the border conflict will undoubtedly be heartily resented by many oldtime Texans, but it is a story which should be told.

Chapter One, is on the whole, exceedingly good. The treatment of the folk ballad of the lower border and the way of life that was developed there is excellent, although you may want to touch it up in view of the new direction of the book. The section on the Anglo-Texan legend about the Mexican is important also, and may represent one of the major contributions of the book. However, I think that I should point out that your case seems to be weakened by a quite understandable note of bitterness and partisanship which creeps in from time to time. I believe that this material can be toned down a little without losing any particular force.

In regard to the references to Dr. Webb's work, both he and I see the point that you are making, and on the whole the point is well made. However, I think that I should point out (without any prompting from Dr. Webb) that it is unfortunate to take a few isolated paragraphs and in effect condemn the work of a man whose writings have in general been characterized by fairness and objectivity. Your position is a little inconsistent in this particular. On the Texan superiority as a whole, and on the other you quote him repeatedly to buttress your tale of Ranger excesses. I think that it is significant to note that your quotation from Webb on page sixteen concerning the Mexican as a merciless and implacable foe is taken from his dissertation and apparently was dropped from the book when he prepared it for publication. However, you must be the final judge of all this. Dr. Webb has enthusiastically recommended your book for publication and he would be the last to squawk because he may be hurt a bit in the process. I merely raise these points for your consideration in the belief that they merit a longer look.

The plan of reorganization which I have suggested may not recommend itself to you. I hold no particular brief for it. I do, however, feel quite strongly that the book must be reorganized with the general reader in mind if it is to achieve its full potentialities. Perhaps you would prefer that it be directed to an audience of professional folklorists without regard to the general reader. In that case, it could be published in something very close to its present form, but it would have to be rather heavily subsidized.[99]

Paredes later said that if he had accepted all of the suggestions "there would be nothing left but a pretty story. I remember telling him, well, if you send it back to me, I can do it."[100] When Paredes was still in El Paso he wrote to his mother telling her that he had received some great news in a letter from The University of Texas Press and that they were interested in publishing his doctoral thesis on Gregorio Cortez. Editors wanted some changes and revisions and Paredes had written back indicating that if they were in agreement on the changes, maybe the book would be published. He ended by writing that the publication would be important for his professional career and his reputation as a scholar.[101] After negotiations, the manuscript was accepted, and it was published on December 29, 1958.

Paredes again wrote to his mother, Cleotilde, about the importance of this event. In a letter dated July 2, 1958, she replied to Américo: "Tengo mucho gusto de tu libro quese publica pronto. Lorenzo te anda haciendo propaganda. Ya te tiene un libro vendido." (I am very glad that your book will be published soon. Lorenzo is advertising your book. He has already sold one book.)[102] Eight days later Américo wrote another letter hoping that Lorenzo, his older brother, could sell some books in Brownsville because 1000 books had to be sold before Paredes would receive royalties.[103]

The tradition at The University of Texas was that when the press published a book, a book signing party would be held at the University Co-op on Guadalupe Street across from the university. The new books would be displayed on a stand. Paredes recalled that his book was treated differently. "Nada, nothing was done for my book. I went there looking for it and I found one copy in the Western Americana section."[104] Initially few copies of the book sold. Soon, however, four hundred copies were purchased by the Texas Folklore Society.

Paredes recalled that when his book was published, "Chicano literature, as such, did not exist, but there was a great deal of writing being done by both Mexicans who had moved to the United States and native Texas Mexicans, which at that time was not recognized... What made the difference was that they write in Spanish and did not have the impact they might have had had they been written in English."[105]

Less than a decade after *With His Pistol in His Hand* was published, the Chicano movement began in California. The changing intellectual climate, the rise of the Black civil rights movement and the slow pace of social, economic, and political reform impacted the creation of "El movimiento" (The Movement). Hundreds of organizations focused on many civil rights issues throughout the country.

In California, César Chávez and Dolores Huerta led the United Farm Workers to champion higher wages and better working conditions. In New Mexico, Reies López Tijerina founded La Alianza Federal de Mercedes (The Federal Alliance of Land Grants) in an attempt to recover lost Mexicano lands. Rodolfo "Corky" Gonzales in Colorado founded the Cruzada Para la Justicia (the Crusade for Justice) to better serve inner city Chicano youth by creating its own school, art gallery, and community center. In Crystal City, Texas, José Angel Gutiérrez founded the Raza Unida Party as a vehicle to help Chicano candidates win school and city council elections. Although it did not achieve its goal of becoming a national independent party, it encouraged Chicanos to participate in the political process.

As the Chicano Movement evolved in California, Chicanos there discovered Paredes' book and began to embrace it. One of these was Tomás Rivera, author of *Y no se lo tragó la tierra*. Rivera, who was then at the University of California at Riverside, claimed that reading *With His Pistol in His Hand*, had encouraged him to write. Some Chicanos indicated to Paredes that the book was important to the movement. The book sold well in California and many Chicanos in Texas heard about the book and began to read it.

This book led to later exchanges with Chicano leaders who respected what Paredes had done for the movimiento. Américo corresponded with a well-known Chicano poet of the era, Alurista (Alberto Baltazar Urista Heredia). Alurista had helped to initiate *Maize: Notebooks of Xicano Art and Literature* to promote Chicano literature.[106] He wrote to Paredes about the work of el Centro Cultural de la Raza at the University of California at San Diego and its funding efforts for publication projects.

The comments and reviews for *With His Pistol in His Hand* were generally positive. George I. Sánchez, professor in the Education Department at The University of Texas at Austin and author of *The Forgotten People*, wrote a letter to the press' director Frank Wardlaw. Sánchez called it "a beautiful work, ... a courageous work of Paredes and of the Press. I congratulate both. It is too, a constructive pioneer job that can lead to spectacular enrichment of Texas culture... This opens horizons in Texas culture only dimly explored in the literature."[107]

History professor Charles C. Cumberland from Michigan State University wrote Paredes in early March 1959 to compliment him on his book. Paredes answered on March 17 thanking him for his kind words and said that the book, he was told, aroused the anger of some people, but only privately. Publicly, it caused little reaction. Paredes wrote,

> I'm afraid that it is not extremely hard to write a book about a Border Mexican lore with documentation that is common. It seems that the standard thing is for the writer to look about himself (rather briefly) and then start writing. If he runs into some problem dealing with research, he just drives across the border, buys a drink at the nearest cantina, and asks the bartender for the right information.[108]

Thomas Sutherland reviewed the book for *The Texas Observer* in February 1959. He described the first half of the book as readable for anyone, except for the friends and relatives of the man shot by Gregorio Cortez. He described the second half as a scholarly study of versions of the Cortez ballad. Sutherland continued, "Paredes has rewritten his doctoral dissertation with commendable enthusiasm and talent."[109]

Gerald Ashford from the *San Antonio Express* wrote a brief but complimentary review in early January 1959. Paredes sent a note to Brownsville native and editor Clarence La Roche indicating that he had liked the review. Ashford replied to Paredes on January 26, 1959, that he would have liked to have written three times as much about this excellent book. He went on to write that the day after the review was published, a grandson of Sheriff Morris called him objecting to the claim in the book that Cortez shot two sheriffs in self-defense. When Ashford advised him to write a letter, he did not. La Roche concluded by writing, "your book is, I think, the most stimulating study of folklore that I have ever read."[110]

W. E. Simeon, in the *Southern Illinois University Journal*, wrote
that *With His Pistol in His Hand* was particularly impressive because of the amount of material on regional folklore it included.
Paredes wrote "with unusual sensitivity and perception about the
injustices suffered by Mexican Americans and how they voiced
their emotions through the *corrido*."[111] A particularly insightful
review was provided by Jimmie Cox, who wrote for the *Fort Worth
Star-Telegram*. He commented, "the quantity of factual material on
the Cortez case has enabled the author to build a credible ac-
count of Cortez' life and the deeds that made him famous... It's
easy to see, from this story, how Gregorio Cortez won such a following among his people. Even the gringos were impressed by the
skill and valor of the wiry Tejano who dared to stand 'with a pistol
in his hand.'"[112]

In the fall of 1958 Paredes returned to The University of Texas at
Austin as an assistant professor of English, and in 1961 he was promoted to associate professor. In 1965 he was promoted to professor
of English and one year later, to professor of anthropology. The publication of his dissertation and his groundbreaking research soon
gained him a regional and national reputation as one of the leading
experts on the corrido. In 1962, Paredes was awarded a Guggenheim
Fellowship, which provided a $10,000 stipend funding his efforts to
collect border folklore. Three years later he became a fellow in the
America Folklore Society.

As part of his Guggenheim study, in September 1962, Paredes
went to Brownsville and northern Mexico to collect corridos and
cuentos (short stories) for his research. Several times while he was in
Mexico, *bandidos* (bandits) attempted to rob him. They placed logs
across the road and came down the mountain with guns. He had
to back down the winding mountain road in his automobile until
he could find a turn-around to escape. He then proceeded to the
small town with his tape recorder and continued to record the ballads and folktales that would eventually appear in his journal articles
and books.[113]

Paredes also collected folksongs with bicultural themes, indicated by the following examples. The first, entitled "Mexicans Who Speak English," is about what he calls the mix or "revoltura" of language along the border.

Los Mexicanos Que Hablan Inglés
En Texas es terrible
por la revoltura que hay,
no hay quién hable castellano,
 nomás puro "goodbye."
Audidú ser, no hay *mai fren*,
 y lo dicen por completo,
 para agarrar el tren
 necesitan sacar boleto.
Luego no fuí pa'l dipo
 a hablar con don Inés,
 yo le hablaba castellano
 y me contestó en inglés.

Para decir diez reales
 dicen *dolái necuora*,
 para decir mañana
 también dicen *tumora.*
Todos queremos hablar
 la idioma americana
 sin poder comprender
 la nuestra castellana.
Yo enamoré a una tejana,
 y de esas de sombrilla,
le dije: "¿Te vas conmigo?"
 Y me dice: "*Luque jia.*"
Yo enamoré a una alemana,
 de esas del garsolé,
le dije: "¿Te vas conmigo?"
Y no dice: "¿*Huachu sei?*"[114]

The Mexicans Who Speak English
(Translation)
In Texas it is terrible
Because of the mixture there
No one speaks Castilian
Just purely "goodbye."
How do you do sir? there is no my friend
And they pronounce it as one
To grab the train
They need to buy a ticket
After I didn't go to the depot
To speak with Don Inés
I speak castellano
He answered in English
To say ten coins
They say a dollar and a quarter
To say tomorrow
They also say tomorrow
We always want to speak
The American language
Without understanding
Our Castilian
I made a tejana fall in love with me
One with an umbrella
I told her "will you go with me?"
She says, "Look here"
I made a German girl fall in love with me
One of many
I told her "will you go with me?"
She doesn't say "what did you say?"

His wife, Nena, however, was unhappy because of his absences
and upset because he did not write as often as she would have liked.
In a letter dated September 1962, she complained:

I still didn't feel like writing to you but I guess I will.
You seem to think that keeping me waiting for 2 days
to hear from you was nothing to get upset about.
Your excuse that it cost more during those days is
just another proof of your penny wise, power fool-
ish ways but, of course, I should be used to your
thoughtless ways…It was just the last straw as far as
I'm concerned…[115]

On one of his research trips to Brownsville at this time, Paredes
stayed with one of his brothers, Amador. He commented that he
had been there for over two days and not been able to use the tape
recorder at all. However, on September 6, Paredes' luck changed, at
least minimally. He wrote,

Morning was more or less a blank, except for a few
side dividends. Eliseo [his oldest brother] told me a
couple of comic anecdotes (which I already had forgotten and must write down) and also got some décimas for him. Also met my "padrino de confirmación"
[godfather of confirmation] whom I had not seen for
about 40 years. The afternoon was luckier. Stopped
to talk with Martin Rutledge "El Lonche" and met an
old schoolmate of mine, Justin McCarty, who turned
out to be a rancho owner now.[116]

One day later, he collected more information and described his activities to

Nena,

This morning went with Amador and met Dr. Magníf-
ico, who turns out to be an Argentino from Córdoba!
How do you like that… Talked to a number of people
there and in the courthouse, where I was told hand-
ful of anecdotes, including a dirty one by the federal
judge H. A. García, old friend. But really good for my
purposes, really shows the Mexican psychology…[117]

On Monday, September 10, Paredes answered a letter that his wife had sent three days earlier. He first responded to her rather cold phone conversations and then described his research of the previous days.

> At all events, I hope that this finds you well, and in a kinder and more Christian mood than you were last Thursday, when I called you on the telephone. I am slowly getting underway here, with the usual frustrations, delay and outpouring of "okane" la "biru" here and there, which I have not been drinking myself… After some false starts, I started recording on Friday night, when Manfred [his nephew] got a few tale-tellers together. Cost me $4 in beer and did get one tape, mostly small talk, and a few good (good and dirty) anecdotes about Mexicans and Americans. The morning of Saturday the 8th I woke up with a terrible stomach ache and a case of the "turistas" (diarrhea)… Went around talking to people with Amador all day Saturday, and buying them beer now and then, feeling terrible…To make matters worse, I found I could not handle the little battery recorder, tape, microphone, extra batteries, etc easily enough to whip them out any old place once somebody got talking. So Saturday was a pretty bad–and– profitless day. That night I was able to down a bowl of soup and feel better. [118]

The next day was even better because the day before, Paredes had purchased a $3 knapsack at Bernie Whitman's Army Surplus Store in which to carry his equipment. He visited two homes, a filling station, and a bar and was able to record those who were in the mood to tell jokes. Sunday had been the most productive day of the trip. In the evening, his brother Amador and his wife Ofelia hosted a dinner attended by friends and family. His eldest brother, Eliseo, recorded three anecdotes, two of which were off-color, and told one himself at the gathering.

Although the separations were difficult at the time, the letters that Paredes wrote to Nena are a rich source of information about his fieldwork. He said that the afternoons and nights were his busiest times because most of his interviewees worked in the morning. The process, however, was much more difficult in 1962 than it was in 1954. Paredes lamented,

> For one thing, many of the old folk have died. For another (perhaps because of the memories of the old recording companies and the desire to become "famous") more people are willing to sing into a mike than to talk into one. Again, people are more likely to sing songs at the spur of the moment, or on demand, than they are likely to tell stories or jokes. Especially for jokes, they have to be in the right mood. Going up to somebody and saying, "Tell me a joke," is like asking somebody, "Say something in English—or Spanish." Again since most of the humor is off-color, there are times when I get the right information in the right mood, but he can't perform because some woman or child joins the group.
>
> This job is like that of a salesman. There are days when things just fall in your lap; there are days when you spend all day seeing people with no results. I am averaging 50 miles a days on my Volks and have not been out of the Brownsville area except for two trips to San Benito, one to Los Laureles (near Los Fresnos) and one to Las Comas... I taped an interview with Nicanor Torres yesterday; he's passed the 100 year mark already. But his age really is telling now. He didn't do much in an hour; his mind wandered, and his voice was weak...[119]

Paredes' humor repeatedly surfaced as he collected jokes and stories in nearby Matamoros. He wrote, "In spite of the heat and the 'turista,' (diarrhea)... which the last had been a blow to my pride, getting it in my own home town... things were not so bad as this morning, when I went to get my tourist card."[120]

His collection of data, however, was rigorous and meticulous. He used the following questionnaire in 1962 and 1963. It is indicative of the detail of his scholarship.

WHAT ROLE DO THE ANGLO-AMERICAN AND HIS CULTURE PLAY IN MEXICAN
FOLKLORE?

    I.   PROSE NARRATIVE.

        1. Do you know any jests or satirical or comic anecdotes in which an Anglo-American is one of the characters?

        2. Do you know any comic stories which depend on a word or phrase in the other language (English or Spanish) for their humor? On a pun between English and Spanish words? On a misunderstanding based on English and Spanish words? In which the whole story is a mixture of English and Spanish?

        3. Have you heard stories about real persons and places in which Anglo-Americans play a part? Stories about ghosts and other supernatural events, sensational crimes, celebrated places, natural features, etc.?

        4. Do you know stories which mention American objects or customs?

        5. Do you know stories which seem to be completely Mexican but which you believe came from the United States and were originally told in English?

    II. SONG (as in prose narrative).

        1. Comic songs with Anglo-American characters.

        2. Comic songs which use both English and Spanish.

        3. Songs with Anglo-American characters that deal with actual persons and events.

        4. Songs which mention American objects or customs.

     5. Songs which may have come from the United States, though they seem to be Mexican.

III. DANCE.

     1. Have American customs or tastes influenced any of the traditional Mexican dances of your area?

     2. Are American dances more popular than Mexican dances today?

IV. GAME.

     1. What kind of games do children play in your neighborhood? Are they in English or Spanish? A mixture of both?

     2. What amusements are most popular with adults?

V. DRAMA.

     1. Are *pastorelas* or other folk plays still common in your area?

     2. Have any American characters been introduced into the folk plays or the dramatic dances of your area?

VI. RITE AND CEREMONY.

     1. Do people still celebrate weddings, baptisms, etc., with as much ceremony as they used to do? Are many things of American or modern manufacture used in the celebrations today?

     2. Have some ceremonies been "Americanized"?

     3. How about funerals and other ceremonies and customs related to the dead?

VII. FESTIVAL.

     1. How much has the celebration of Christmas changed in recent years?

     2. Do you know any other festivals influenced by Anglo-American customs?

VIII. BELIEF AND PRACTICE.

     1. Do you know any popular beliefs, taken seriously or not, about Americans? That they are lucky or unlucky, that their big feet stink, etc.?

2. What beliefs and customs of Anglo-Americans seem queer to you?
3. Has the Mexican way of doing things changed much because of influence from the United States?

IX. SPEECH AND SPEECH FORMALS.

1. What names do you know for North Americans? What is their origin?
2. Are there gestures or other signs to ridicule or identify Americans?
3. Formulas, curses, boasts, mock prayers, tags or labels ridiculing Americans?
4. Proverbs, proverbial expressions or comparisons doing the same thing?
5. Riddles using both languages or making fun of Americans?
6. Is the Spanish that you hear daily becoming more Americanized?[121]

Paredes was considerably frustrated by the Mexican "system" of customs. On one trip he cleared his camera and recorder through American customs with some delay but not too much difficulty. At Mexican customs, however, he faced several obstacles. He had to "tip" the girl one dollar for filling out his car permit. She told Paredes that his recording equipment was not included in the permit because it was not necessary. He then drove to the office next to hers and the inspector took the permit from Paredes, pointed to the camera and recorder and asked what they were. When Américo related what the girl had said, the inspector unpleasantly answered "no" and told him to see the chief. Paredes refused and walked to the girl's office who seemed surprised.

Paredes kept his eye on his Volkswagen while someone was placing tourist stickers on it. The inspector came out and "thrust" the car permit into Paredes' hand and said, "¡Tenga! Llevéselo así" (Here! Take it as it is). Paredes later wrote,

So the whole thing was clear. It meant that every time
I crossed the river I would be stopped and badgered
until I gave out with some sizeable mordida (bribe).
I wouldn't be surprised if they didn't phone immediately to the "garita" (guard house), to be on the wait
for me. I drove to Eliseo's, feeling mad enough to turn
around and go back home to Austin. But he called
General González Treviño, the customs chief, and
we went to the main customs office where the good
general had one of his subchiefs add the camera and
recorders to my car permit. According to him they
belonged there; that is to say the inspector was right.
I just wonder what happens to people who do not
have the right brother and the right connections.[122]

During his stay in Brownsville, Paredes also wrote letters to his
children. In one letter to Alan, he commented about the heat and
the humidity in Brownville while he stayed with his brother Amador.
Paredes also inquired about Alan's new school in Austin and asked
him to help his mother around the house. He asked if Julie had
said any new words. Obviously, Paredes wished that he were with his
family: "I miss you all very much, even though I spend the whole day
meeting people and talking to them."[123]

Throughout the 1960s Paredes taught at various institutions as a
visiting professor. In the summer of 1961 and 1962 he taught Latin
America Area Studies at West Virginia University. In 1967, he taught
anthropology at the University of California at Berkeley.

In a letter to his wife, Paredes described his experiences at Berkeley. In addition to indicating that there was much adjustment and
preparation, his letter also revealed a glimpse of California campus
life during that decade.

Immediately after I went out on the U.C. equiva-
lent of the Mall, where they hold demonstrations, and
you would never guess what I saw. A big bearded student going the length of the area... on a unicycle!

I have no classes today and spent sometime in the library doing some work on *Folktales of Mexico.* Then to the office for a moment—I thought —but immediately was waylaid by students. At lunch today a Chinese student sitting opposite me asked me if I thought architecture should have spiritual values and before I knew it we got into a long and friendly discussion. The students here are much more awake— there is no doubt about that.[124]

By 1967, Américo and Amelia had three children: Alan, Vince, and Julia. Amelia has been described by her son Vince as an enabler because she cared for the Paredes children when Américo was away as a visiting professor, conducting research, or presenting his research at conferences throughout North America and Europe. Especially difficult for them was the diagnosis in 1963 that Julie, their daughter, was mentally ill. Américo and Nena took Julie to Ann Arbor, Michigan, for two weeks of observation and evaluation. Paredes believed that the trip was a waste of time because observations on her were conducted by an employee of the school and not by psychiatrists. He believed they were more interested in compiling data for their research than in her well-being. They told Américo and Amelia what they already knew, that Julie suffered from a type of childhood schizophrenia. To him psychiatrists seemed uninterested. Paredes articulated his feelings in a letter to Lorenzo, his brother.

And since they did no real diagnosis I was particularly enraged when the little doctor—casi un mocoso el peladito [almost a snotnose kid, the little jerk]— brutally told us that "since our name was not Rockefeller" we should expect Julie to spend her life in the state hospital. Nada más porque Nena es muy fuerte se pudo mantener sin llorar hasta que ya estábamos en la carretera pues subimos inmediatamente. A veces me daban ganas en el camino de dejar que se fuera el carro en contra de algún puente, en tal estado salimos de Ann Arbor. [Only because Nena was very strong was she able to keep from crying until we were already on the highway, as we left immediately. There were times on the road that I wanted to let the car hit against a bridge; in that state we left Ann Arbor].[125]

He recalled that they did not know what to do and were in a state of shock for a few weeks. They did nothing except attempt to get back to normal. Paredes was trying to catch up with his academic work and he and Nena were on tranquilizers. They hoped to enroll Julie at the Austin State School.[126] Vince Paredes later commented, "As for Julie's condition, Dad took the pain and kept it in. Mother took on the issue and did something about it."[127]

Throughout most of her marriage to Américo, Amelia was a tireless advocate for the mentally retarded. She strove to better their lives by campaigning to improve state schools and working with the Texas legislature to better fund and improve Texas State Schools. She was a valued member of the Human Rights Advisory Committee of the Austin State School, a charter member of the Parent Association for the Retarded of Texas, and President of the Austin State School Parent Association.[128]

It was not easy for Nena to run the household and for Américo to be away from his family. An insight into their thoughts about being away from each other can possibly be seen in their letters. While teaching at West Virginia University Paredes wrote, "[I] can hardly wait to see all of you, and that little girl [Julie] that gets into the bathtub all by herself now. Give my love to the boys. Tell Tito [Vince] that I miss him a lot and to be good. Tell Alan that I am proud of his acting. And tell him that I wish he could help around the house more. And tell Gusai [Julie] I love her."[129]

It was evident that although Nena supported Américo's academic travels, she was not always happy about their time apart. In a January 28, 1967, letter to her husband, who was at the University of California at Berkeley, her frustration is evident: "All I've had from you is a measly postcard that came today. The children are well, Julie seems all right but has had trouble going to sleep and night before last I had to hold her hand before she went to sleep... If this letter seems disjointed it's because I write a letter and then go do something else... I hope I get a long letter from you Monday. I hope you get something out of this because I like it less everyday."[130]

Vince Paredes, their younger son, conveyed an interesting personal insight into their marriage, which he characterized as both traditional and modern. He remembered,

> My mother stayed home and my father would work. That's where it ended as far as tradition. My mother was much of my father's career. She deserves a lot of the credit. She had intelligence and drive. Since my sister is retarded, she took that issue on not only to give her a decent life for my sister, but to address all the issues about how retarded people are treated and cared for. She did something about it directly.[131]

He continued by saying that both had initiative and both were action-oriented. His father would tell him that when there were disagreements or arguments, Amelia would win most of them.[132] Vince also remembered that they were avid photographers and much of their married life was documented in photographs. They also enjoyed working on crossword puzzles. "The two had lively discussions about letters that my mom would send to the editor because my dad would try to edit them before she sent them."[133] Amelia, who could write quite well, did not appreciate Américo's attempts to edit her works.

Paredes loved his wife and his children very much. Vince, currently a vice president of an Austin-based educational software company, recalled what life was like in the Paredes household. He said that Christmas was the big event of the year and that the family ate tamales and eggs on Christmas morning. His father stressed the importance of family meals. Vince commented, "I remember having to sit down as a family for breakfast and dinner. That was an important thing to him. Now that I look back, those were things that I think are special now, that I remember about our family."[134]

The young Paredes explained that his father was a perfectionist who made him want to answer his own question by first researching it, then accumulating evidence for it and finally answering it. There were tasks, however, that even Américo Paredes could not do, although he tried. One of these was to be a repairman around the house. Vince remembers that his "Dad tried to be a handyman, but it didn't always work out... We painted the house once; that was an experience."[135] Paredes, however, enjoyed yard work. In the backyard, he planted a fig tree and what he called his victory garden. He pulled weeds, sodded the grass, and picked the fruit. He was especially proud of his tomatoes.

Vince also remembered traveling with his father or driving to visit him. Some trips were lengthy. For example, Américo's family visited him at the University of West Virginia in Morgantown when he was a visiting professor there. The trips they took to Brownsville would begin at three o'clock in the morning before it became unbearably hot. The car was not air conditioned and the drive seemed endless.

In many ways, Américo Paredes was a traditional father. Vince reminisced about growing up as the son of Dr. Américo Paredes,

> When we were young he was very affectionate. I remember him tucking me in at night, holding his hand across campus. Once we got to a certain age, it was more "you're a man now." Once I got to a certain point, Alan actually talked to him more. Once I became a young man, then I was expected to act like one... I didn't talk to him a lot about what was going on in my life; when there was something I needed, he was real open.[136]

Paredes always emphasized the importance of an education to his children. College was something he wanted for all of them. It was expected. Vince said that his father paid his tuition and books throughout his undergraduate and graduate studies. When the film *With His Pistol in His Hand* was released, the proceeds were divided among the children to help defray the costs of their college education.[137]

Paredes expected not only a great deal from those around him, but also a great deal from himself. Vince reiterated that his father was a perfectionist who demanded that his children work to the best of their abilities. He did not, however, verbalize it. Vince recalls, "It's nothing that was ever said. It was purely by example. Anything from mowing the lawn to studying to solving an algebra equation. His work ethic is obvious in who he was and in his work."[138]

Vince said that his father enjoyed a good argument and a good discussion with his colleagues at the university and with his own family at home. Often, at the kitchen table, Américo would listen to the boys and consider their arguments and then decide. Vince then made an interesting comment about his father's writing: "I don't know if he enjoyed writing as much as he felt he had to get things out. He wanted to accomplish certain things. What he enjoyed about being a professor was the academic and social interaction."[139] On many occasions, Paredes invited his colleagues and students to his home to sing songs or celebrate academic achievements. Mexican holidays and Américo's own birthday were also festive occasions. Those young academics in attendance later became the Paredes-trained scholars who continue to affect Chicano Studies today. Among them were José Limón, Manuel Peña, Ricardo Romo, and Ramón Saldívar.

Parents of Américo, Justo and Cleotilde Manzano Paredes

Américo playing guitar outside his Brownsville home

Américo the young poet during the 1930s

Américo in a suit in his 20s

Américo in the onion field along the border

Américo in his late 20s in Brownsville

Américo with guitar during the first Charro Days parade in 1938

Américo in military uniform after World War II

Américo playing the guitar with army friends in Japan in 1946

Américo as a young journalist in post-war Japan

Newlyweds Américo and Nena in post-World War II Asia

Américo and Nena in Japan in 1948

Américo and Nena on the Japanese coastline in 1949

Américo in his thirties strumming a guitar

Américo after receiving his Ph.D in 1956

Américo, father, with young sons Alan and Vincent
on UT-Austin campus in 1955

Américo and his "victory garden" grapevine in 1965

Américo, the young professor, in a classroom at the University of Texas at Austin during the 1960s

Américo on a northern Mexico rancho in 1963

Américo doing field research in northern Mexico in the mid 1960s

Professor Paredes during the early 1970s

Professor Paredes with longtime secretary and
friend Francis Terry at his retirement party at UT in 1984

Américo, UT Professor, displaying recent awards during the early 1980s

Professor Américo in Austin at the age of 81

Professors Américo Paredes and Rolando Hinojosa at Américo's home
celebrating Américo's 80th birthday

Américo Paredes in his early 80s at Parlin Hall
where he worked most of his career

Américo and Nena on their 50th wedding anniversary in 1998

Vince and author releasing Américo's and Amelia's ashes at the mouth of
the Río Grande in November 1999

CHAPTER FIVE

A PROFESSOR OF LEGENDARY STATUS

Throughout his professional life, Américo Paredes received numerous awards. He responded to the accolades with his usual dignity, but Vince remembered that his father never talked about the importance of an award. The Order of the Aztec Eagle was significant, but he saw it more as an opportunity to be heard. There was one recognition that he especially valued, however. Near the end of his life on November 26, 1998, he was given a tribute in his hometown at his first college, Brownsville Junior College, now The University of Texas at Brownsville/Texas Southmost College. Paredes was proud to be from Brownsville and he was proud to be recognized by the college that he attended. In that sense, he was happy to receive the award.[140]

Vince remembered, "my father was a teacher first, then a scholar. He might not have separated those in his mind because he was teaching people to be scholars. Those things weren't separated. He presented his whole self to everybody and his family. He was the same person to me and his colleagues."[141] In the 1960s, his scholarly research produced numerous articles, reviews, and books. It also gave him enough institutional leverage to found the Center for Mexican American Studies at The University of Texas at Austin in 1970.

Américo Paredes was a professor extraordinaire. Although he was one of the most demanding instructors on campus, students filled his classes. An examination of two of Paredes' syllabi document the rigor of his courses. One of the many courses he taught was Materials and Methods of Folklore Research, a survey of folklore theory and method from the 1700s to the present. The required reading included five textbooks and four reports. The course was organized into weekly seminars for which the topics were coordinated by a class member who was required to have a comprehensive command of the subject under discussion. Additionally, the students were required to write twelve papers of at least five pages in length on weekly topics and a fifteen-page paper critiquing a recently published book on folklore. Oral presentations focusing on the research were also required.

The graduate syllabus for his folklore classes clearly indicated his substantial expectations for folklore majors and anthropology students who had a concentration in the area of folklore. His Reference Tools section (bibliographies, catalogs, dictionaries, and journals) numbered 47 pages. That was followed by a detailed section on Theory and Method, including texts, essays, articles, history of folkloristic thought, and fieldwork. The following section on genres included everything from religion, curing, and magic to folktales, myths, songs, riddles, and proverbs. Paredes expected his students to master the information and to be able to articulate in both oral and written form.[142]

Throughout his lengthy teaching career, Paredes taught thousands of students from the United States and abroad. Many remembered him for his knowledge but many remembered him for his dedication beyond the classroom. One letter dated June 27, 1971, was from a young artist named Carmen Lomas Garza, who was requesting information from Américo. Garza was working on an altar project and about to transfer from Texas A & I University in Kingsville, Texas, to The University of Texas at Austin. She wrote,

> I am trying to look for materials that will help me specifically with material art rather than oral art. From your paper "Suggestions," I have picked out a few books that I will try to get from the A & I library... I

would like more suggestions for more books, articles, etc. that will help me with this project..... Now it is important that I finish this work, hoping that it will help me become a better person, thus a better artist.[143]

His expectations increased considerably for his graduate students. At times his comments about their work seemed unrelenting. On June 23, 1982, he sent a letter to doctoral student Jim McNutt about his study on folklorists of the Southwest and what Américo criticized as a lack of objectivity. In his dissertation McNutt used J. Frank Dobie's criticism of the grammar in a *corrido* stanza. Paredes pointed out that Dobie "was wrong on even more fundamental grounds" apparently thinking that *gente* was the subject of *junto* and *estuvieron*, "but that was not the case. There are many examples of nonstandard usage in the *corridos*, but this is not one of them."[144]

About Chapter 7 of McNutt's dissertation, Paredes commented that "this, to my mind, is the weakest part of your work, and more because of the difficulties inherent in the subject than anything else ... I had hoped not to take up those things with anyone, but the results of your study are so skewed that something must be said about it, even though it enhances nobody's image in the process."[145]

McNutt revised his dissertation, completed his studies, and, like many of Paredes' former students, befriended his former teacher. Paredes, of course, was delighted with his student's success. After McNutt was named director of the North Carolina Museum of History, Paredes wrote to congratulate him and to say that "it was about time you moved to that sort of position."[146]

In the classroom, Paredes was soft-spoken but imposing because of his scholarly reputation and because he expected his students to complete their assignments at their highest capacity. Rolando Hinojosa has been an English professor and writer at The University of Texas at Austin for over thirty years. In 1984, he moved into the office that Américo Paredes had occupied for many years at Parlin Hall. Over the years, he met many of Paredes' ex-students. Hinojosa commented,

To date, I've not met one who, upon our own home meetings, fails to mention Américo Paredes in glowing terms; not all peaches and cream at first, they agree, since he piled them with what they termed an unbelievable amount of work week after week. They're grateful, however, for he taught them discipline and the rejection of or settling for the second rate.[147]

Antonio Zavaleta, a professor of anthropology and former Vice-President for External Affairs at The University of Texas at Brownsville, arrived at The University of Texas in 1970. He became one of the first graduate students in the Anthropology Department there. He and his fellow students were impressed by Paredes' dedication to the border culture even before he acquired a national reputation. It was a time when there were fewer than one hundred Hispanic doctoral candidates in the United States. Zavaleta recalls, "The effect he had on his students was hypnotic. His approval was a validation of us and our work ... His stature came after he began influencing us to have pride in ourselves, to become accomplished in our fields before he achieved legendary status and transcended simple academic popularity."[148] Zavaleta continued by saying that Paredes was a *sembrador*, a planter of seeds. The fruits of those seeds have blossomed at other schools and universities in the Southwest and are the scholars and professors who pass on their knowledge to their own students.

José Limón, the current director of the Center for Mexican Studies at The University of Texas at Austin, knew Paredes for over three decades. Limón was his student, his assistant, his colleague, and his friend. According to Limón, Paredes defined "Mexicanidad" at its best. He was more than a teacher and dissertation supervisor. Limón remembers, "for me, he became something else; a kind of living symbol of rectitude; of what is correct; of consummate integrity. He was an example for the way that men and women ought to conduct themselves in public and even in private...Era muy fino [He was very refined.]"[149]

Richard Flores, currently an anthropology professor at The University of Texas at Austin, remembers the first time he met his future professor. Flores was a first-year graduate student attending the fall reception banquet hosted by the Center for Mexican American Studies. He remembered when Paredes walked into the room: "Here was this giant of an intellectual figure, but so unassuming, so nice, so approachable ... Perhaps the premier intellectual Chicano scholar that I had ever met ... I was really surprised."[150] Flores describes Paredes' classes as very demanding. When he received the syllabus for the course entitled Mexican Popular Culture, the Corrido and the Décima, he was stunned. The reading list was "amazing" and he remembers going home to his wife and asking how he was going to get it all done, but he did because that is what Paredes expected of his students.[151]

Flores emphasized that Dr. Paredes taught beyond the classroom because part of what he taught was the honesty with which one approaches one's work. One significant lesson Flores learned was that the material and culture must be mastered well to avoid repeating mistakes made by the past generation. He was a professor, a mentor, and a role model.[152]

Beverly J. Stoeltje, a member of the first class of folklore graduate students, was advised to enroll in Dr. Paredes' Décima, Corrido, and Copla class. When she was called on to present the first reading, she was shocked. Paredes later explained to her that he expected her to have some knowledge of the subject because she had taken an undergraduate class. This first interaction set a precedent for his teaching. By conducting his classes with dignity, addressing his students formally, and assuming a serious commitment, he set high expectations for all of the folklore program.[153]

Emilio Zamora, associate professor in the School of Information and the Department of History is, like Paredes, a Valley native. His specialty is Mexican-American history. He remembers taking a course with Paredes entitled The History of Thought in Mexico Regarding the Important Question About Who the Mexican Is. In this one-to-one class, Zamora was made aware of Paredes' broad understanding of Mexican culture and history. Zamora states, "He was very knowledgeable about the literature in which Mexican philosophers and historians determined who the Mexican was. As an historian who has a special interest in the recovery of our historical record, I'm particularly interested in the record he left for us."[154] Zamora was pensive as he spoke about how Paredes should be remembered. He said that his memory should invoke the following: his achievements as an academic and an important leader of the Mexicano origin people; his presentation of our experiences, our interests and our concerns in his work and our claim to him; and his embodiment of values such as work ethic, principles and a sense of responsibility to his community.[155]

José Angel Gutiérrez, Chicano activist, author, attorney, and currently a professor of political science at The University of Texas at Arlington, offered an insight into how Paredes impacted his life. Gutiérrez recalls,

> Don Américo rescued me. He was my lifesaver. I started the Ph.D. program in government at UT Austin in 1968 after I had just finished my Masters at St. Mary's in San Antonio. But Vietnam caught me and I had to quit my program. In '70 I applied and was accepted in the government program at UT Austin again but I found out that Don Américo had founded a Mexican American Studies program. I applied through that for a Ph.D. and got it through his program.[156]

While Gutiérrez pursued his doctoral studies, he was asked to teach a Chicano politics class. Soon, his lectures became so controversial that the government faculty and the administrators no longer wanted him there. Even the FBI came to visit the administrators to suggest that Gutiérrez be removed. To accomplish that, the university offered him a scholarship. Shortly after the offer, according to Gutiérrez, "Don Américo and I had a heart-to-heart, macho-a-macho conversation about whether principles or the Ph.D. was more important than my teaching at that moment. Y pues yo andaba muerto de hambre [and I was starving], so I took the scholarship."[157]

Gutiérrez received his doctorate with the assistance and advice of Dr. Paredes and he has never forgotten that. "He was my mentor. He was my scholar and, of course, his writings impacted me. He was truly a Chicano scholar and a don."[158]

Paredes' reputation as a scholar was as impressive as his reputation in the classroom. His articles and stories appeared in the *American Quarterly*, *The Texas Observer*, the *Journal of American Folklore*, and numerous other journals. Topics included history, folklore, and folk music. In 1960, one of his articles on culture appeared in *The Texas Observer*. It was entitled "The Mexican Contribution to Our Culture." Paredes began by stating that prejudice, ignorance, and hostility have historically made English-speaking writers slight or ignore the Mexican contribution to the American Southwest. However, ignorance about culture has not been limited solely to the Anglos. Average Mexican Americans know little about their own background and are sometimes apologetic about what they do know. He remarked that the Mexican contribution to the Southwest is significant and is evident all around us in songs, foods, and stories. Historic figures such as the vaqueros and Spanish language contributions to American English are also important additions. Paredes concluded,

> We can justly call the Southwest our own; we can look back with pride at the part our Mexican forebears played in its evolution. It is part of us, made up as it is of so many different peoples and with so many points of view that have here met and mingled into something worthy of being valued, something that is our own.[159]

As the 1960s continued, so did Paredes' scholarship and creative output. Over forty of his publications and reviews appeared in scholarly journals. In 1961 he translated the Edward Tinker book *Corridos and Calaveras: Mirror of the Mind of the People*. In 1964 he translated *Of American Extremes* written by Daniel Cosío Villegas. One year later, he co-authored a book about guitar music entitled *Folk Music of Mexico* with Joseph Castle. One particular story, "The Hammon and the Beans," appeared in the April 1963 issue of *The Texas Observer.* It was a story that Paredes had written when he was young and chronicled an event during his childhood. Américo had befriended a little girl who suddenly died and left him with many unanswered questions.

The story about the story is equally fascinating. Paredes wrote "The Hammon and the Beans" in 1959 when he completed his novel *George Washington Gómez.* Both are set near historic Fort Brown, which was originally established in 1846 to protect the South Texas border. Lorenzo Paredes, Paredes' older brother, recalled what Américo had told him about "The Hammon and the Beans." In 1920 when Américo was five years old and living on Harrison Street near Fort Brown, he met a little girl. One day she was playing outside, and Américo began to play with her and they became friends. He could not remember her name, but he did remember that she used to climb a wooden fence in the backyard and walk on the board near the top. He also noticed that she would also go inside her house and return with a plate. She proceeded to the wire fence at Fort Brown and put the plate on the ground. The child then went through the fence and went to the mess hall where the soldiers were eating. She came out holding the plate in both hands. When Américo saw her again, he asked her why she went to the fort. She said because the soldiers gave her "hammon" and she would bring it home to her mother. The soldiers each gave her a teaspoon of ham.

One day, Américo went out to play with her, but she wasn't there. A second and third day passed before Américo went to the girl's house to ask her mother about his friend. She replied that she had died and Américo went home without saying a thing.[160] Lorenzo continued, "that is the girl that he mentioned in 'The Hammon and the Beans'; that girl stayed in his head."[161]

Américo had submitted the story for a short story contest in high school, but failed to win even honorable mention. After appearing in *The Texas Observer* it was subsequently published in other journals and years later in literature textbooks. About *The Hammon and the Beans and Other Stories,* in 1994 Paredes commented, "The path of the publication, however, was not an easy one. I did try to get it published because 'no importa tan arrancados que estabamos' [no matter how broke we were], we still would have enough for an envelope and a stamp with a story that took only two or three pages ... I got it back; there was never anyone interested in that."[162]

When Paredes returned from the Far East to study and to teach at The University of Texas at Austin, he again submitted the story for publication and again it was rejected. Sometimes the editors would be polite enough to say a few words. Their response was, "we would like to see more of Chonita." Paredes later commented, "they wanted the story to be cute, you know ... I try to think of her as a kind of Emma Tenayuca (San Antonio labor organizer) who had not shown her promise."[163]

In 1963, Paredes also published "The Ancestry of Mexico's Corridos: A Matter of Definition" in the *Journal of American Folklore.* Here he responded to an article written by Merle E. Simmons implying that Paredes had not properly understood the evolution of the corrido. Paredes insisted that the difference of opinion was one mostly of terminology. In a scholarly, yet firm manner Paredes ended with a comment indicating that neither he or Simmons was right or wrong and because folk theories, like other theories, were always based on incomplete data. Paredes wrote, "The fact that we cannot even agree on a definition of folktale is notorious. We lack a language of our own; not necessarily a pseudoscientific jargon but simply a clear definition of terms, so we can understand each other. This is a problem that we must halfway solve before we have any right to the name of 'science,' which we so often bestow upon our favorite subject."[164]

Paredes continued his scholarship throughout the mid-1960s. In 1965, several of his publications appeared in journals. "El cowboy norteamericano en el folklore y la literatura" ("The American Cowboy in Folklore and Literature") appeared in *Cuadernos del Instituto Nacional de Antropología,* a Buenos Aires publication. That same year the article appeared in The University of Texas Institute of Latin American Studies Offprint Series.

In 1967, his short story "The Hammon and the Beans" reappeared in the *Southwest Writers Anthology* edited by Martin Shockley. Within the year Paredes founded and directed the Center of Intercultural Studies in Folklore and Oral History at The University of Texas at Austin. He considered his work here one of his most significant achievements. "The Décima on the Texas-Mexican Border" was published as No. 54 of The University of Texas Institute of Latin America Studies Offprint Series in 1968. It was a reprint of two earlier articles from the *Journal of the Folklore Institute.*

That same year Paredes published an article in the *Handbook of Latin America Studies.* It was entitled "Special Article: A Selective Annotated Bibliography of Recent Works in Latin America Folklore, 1960–1967." That same year his "Folk Medicine and the Intercultural Jest" appeared in *Spanish-Speaking People in the United States,* the proceedings from the Annual Spring Meeting of the American Ethnological Society in Seattle. Paredes began by explaining that this was a discussion of six jests or *tallas* collected in Spanish, but translated to English for the presentation. They were collected in Brownsville, Texas, in 1962 and 1963 as part of several hundred recordings during the various field trips described in the previous chapter. His goal was to relate the riddles (*adivinanzas*) to Texas Mexican attitudes toward cultural change and to Anglo Americans. The common theme of the six stories is that there is a sick person and people who seek a cure for him. The first five include folk healing remedies. Number six does not include a *curandero* or faith healer, but does include the recommendation of a wrong purgative to the person who is sick.[165]

The fourth story is a humorous example of a girl who "has a Mexican disease."

> This is something they say happened in Mission or McAllen or somewhere over there, in Hidalgo County, you see? A girl began to feel very sick in the stomach, and they took her to the doctor. And the doctor

said, "This girl has appendicitis." He said, "We'll have to take out her appendix, no other way. If she isn't feeling better by tomorrow at ten," he said, "I'll come for her."

So then a woman said, "Look," she said, "Don Pedrito is in town. He's a curandero," she said, "and he's a very wise old man." He said, "What for?"

"He never goes around recommending operations," she said, "and he never makes a mistake."

Well, so they called him. He said, "Let's see, let's see," he said. "What does the doctor say?"

"Oh, the doctor says it's her appendix."

He said, "Oh, no. Those doctors are a bunch of *cabrones* [billy goats, tricksters]; all they know is about diseases in English. But this little girl is sick in the Mexican way; she has a Mexican disease," he said. "And it can be only one of three things: bled flesh, bruised blood, or a blocked fart."

Este es un caso que dicen que pasó en Mission o McAllen o por acá, aquí en Hidalgo, ves? Una muchacha que comenzó a estar muy mala del estómago y la llevaron con el doctor y el doctor dijo:

—Esta muchacha tiene apendicitis.—Dijo—Hay que sacarle el apéndice, no hay más. Si para mañana a las diez de las mañana no se le corta—dijo—, yo vengo por ella.

Y ya entonces dijo una señora:—Mire—dijo—, aquí está don Pedrito. Es un curandero—dijo—y —Para qué? —dijo.

—Ese nunca anda recomendando operaciones—dijo—y es muy acertado.

Pues ya lo trajeron. Dijo:—A ver, a ver —dijo—, qué dice el doctor?

—Pues el doctor dice que es el apéndice.

Dijo:—No, hombre. Estos doctores cabrones nomás saben ellos las enfermedades en inglés. Pero esta muchachita tiene una enfermedad en el mexicano. Esta es enfermedad Mexicana —dijo—y debe de ser, de tres cosas una: carne juida, sangre molida o pedo detenido.

-Informant no. 24[166]

In 1968, Paredes hired Frances Terry as his secretary. They would work together for the next two decades. She became a valued co-worker and family friend. Ms. Terry recalled that she had just completed business school and was looking for a job. She came into Paredes' office for the interview. At the time, she knew little about academics, but Paredes saw her potential and hired her. Frances remembered that "you could just feel the power when he walked into the room."[167] She typed his syllabi in English and often typed his books and letters in Spanish, although she did not know the language. Paredes expected perfection and taught Terry the three P's: professionalism, punctuality, and perfection. Terry recalls,

> Everything had to be just right. He had an unbeliev-
> able mind. He was just fantastic. I had never seen any-
> body that could think like he thought and write like
> he wrote. He was never tired. He was always enthusi-
> astic about what he did…he'd come in and ask me to
> type a chapter or whatever he was working on for an
> article. By the time he gave it to me he had already
> typed it on a manual typewriter. He very seldom had
> any corrections.[168]

During the many years she worked with Paredes, Frances Terry developed an understanding of how he interacted with his students. She said they enjoyed their relationship with him. Like his students themselves, Terry believed that he taught his pupils the lesson of tough love. Paredes sometimes gave them a thousand pages a week to read. Students on occasion spent the night in the library because there was a suite at the end of the hall in the Student Resource Building. At times, they became frustrated because he required so much reading, but when they completed his course, they were well prepared. They loved him. He treated everyone equally and people around him knew they were his family. Many later were hired at research universities. Ms. Terry concluded by saying that Américo taught her how to effectively interact with people.[169]

Before the end of the decade, he was selected as the U.S Representative on the Comité de Folklore for the Organization of American States. This was a prestigious appointment that Paredes took seriously and used it to promote the field.

During the 1960s Paredes also served as editor of several scholarly journals. For the first half of the decade, he was an editorial board member and bibliographer for the *Southern Folklore Quarterly*. In 1964 and 1965 he was the book review editor for the *Journal of American Folklore*. From 1966 to 1968, Paredes served on the editorial board for *Folklore Americas*. In 1968 he was a contributing editor for the *Handbook of Latin American Studies*. From 1968 to 1973 he was the editor for the *Journal of American Folklore*. In 1970, he became editor of The University of Texas American Folklore Series.

The decade of the 1970s was as memorable for Américo Paredes as the previous decade. He emerged as one of most prolific, insightful, and respected folklorists and scholars in the country. The decade began with the publication of *Folktales of Mexico* (1970) and his founding of the Center for Mexican Studies at UT-Austin.

Folktales is a collection of folktales translated from the Spanish and edited by Paredes. In the foreword, Professor Richard Dorson comments about Américo's intuitive research in Mexico:

> In this country of striking contrasts, the first of consequence in the New World to feel the European conqueror's heel, the folklorist finds his ideal laboratory. Here he sees within one nation the uncertain balance between the high civilization and the village culture, and he recognizes that no observer can comprehend

the whole without knowing something of both parts
... In Mexico the folk communities flourish twenty
kilometers off the highways and extend into the mes-
tizo population of the cities.[170]

Beginning with a history of folklore studies and folklore societies
in Mexico, Paredes asserts that the first Mexican folktales may have
existed before the fall of the Aztecs in Tenochtitlán. Bernal Díaz del
Castillo, soldier to Cortés, left evidence of some folktales including
one about Cortés' companion and interpreter Doña Marina or La
Malinche. Paredes then surveys Mexican and Mexican American
folktales up to 1970 and comments about genuine folk narratives
and those tales that were of a dubious folk style. He argues that folktale collections should include where each folktale was collected
and the relevant background information on sources employed. Additionally, he adds that to validate the collections, features such as
sources, style, and annotated texts should also be included.

The meticulous collection of information for the text and the
validation of the folklore in it are evident throughout Paredes' book.
The following is an example of the traditional tale of the banshee or
witch wife, from *Folktales of Mexico*. Note that it concludes with information about where it was collected and from whom, serving as an
example of Paredes' own advice to other folklorists.

THEY SAY THAT in the Náhualtl-speaking district of San Cristóbal Las Casas there lived a man and
his wife. The woman was a witch and she was deceiving her husband. It was her custom to say some magic
words that made the flesh drop from her bones, leaving nothing but the skeleton. Then she would sprout
wings, and the skeleton would go out flying though
the air. In this shape she would go out every night
and frighten people out at late hours.

When her husband found out she was deceiving
him and that her skeleton went out every night, he
decided to punish her. One night he lay awake in bed,

pretending he was asleep. He heard noises as his wife got out of bed and went out into the street. He got up too and followed her. Hiding in the shadows he saw how the flesh dropped from his wife's bones and how wings sprouted from her skeleton. Then he saw her fly away, making a noise like bones falling apart. When he got over his fright, he went where the flesh was, and he chopped it up into bits with his machete. Then he sprinkled salt over it so it would die. Then he went back and hid in a corner and waited for the skeleton to return.

When this took place the skeleton stood before the flesh and said the words to make it come back in place. But the flesh did not obey because it was dead. The despairing skeleton flew away. Many are the people who see this being flying through the air at night, and they say it announces somebody's death.[171]

Localized legend. Principal motifs:E574, "Appearance of ghost as death omen"; G229.I.I, "Witch who is out of skin is prevented from reentering it when person salts or peppers skin"; G250.I, "Man discovers his wife is a witch."

Another story of witchcraft widespread in the Greater Mexican area. Compare J. M. Espinosa, no. 83 and Foster, "Sierra Popoluca Folklore," no.14. In the Foster text the witch is the husband instead of the wife. He is turned over to the authorities and is burned alive.

See also Brinton, *Essays*, p. 171.[172]

One of the anecdotes collected by Paredes in Matamoros was "The Miraculous Mesquite" collected from an "unmarried female informant in her late fifties" identified by the initials G.T.G.

THIS WAS A MAN who was very bad to his wife, somewhere in the back country. He beat her every day, terrible beatings that left her all black and blue. Life was hell for the poor thing. And sometimes she said, "Oh, I wish he would die so I could get some rest."

So one day he had a fit and fell down like dead. They put him in the coffin, held a wake, prayed over him. And early next day they took him out to bury him, on the shoulders of four rancheros from the village. The coffin was a just a poor box, and they wouldn't put the lid on it until they got to the cemetery.

As the body left the house, the widow began to tear her hair and scream, for this was what she was supposed to do, no matter how happy she was to see him dead now. Just then, as they were passing with the box under a mesquite, the man woke up from the fit he had. So he sat up in the box and grabbed hold of a branch of the mesquite, a branch that was hanging low.

At this they put the box on the ground and took him out; they cared for him, and he ended up hale and hearty. So he went on as before, drinking and beating his wife. And so on for a few months, until he had another fit that was the real thing. Well, this time the wake lasted three days, until the body began to smell. But no. This time he was good and dead.

Well, so they take him out on their shoulders once more, and the widow began to cry and yell the same as the first time. But she was watching where they carried the body through the yard, and now and then she would stop crying and yell at them [weepy voice], "Don't take him under the mesquite! Don't take him under the mesquite!"[173]

The eighty-five collected pieces that comprise *Folktales of Mexico* include legendary narratives, animal tales, folktales, jokes and anecdotes, and formula tales from rural areas on the U.S. side of the border to narratives and folktales from modern and traditional Mexico. P. Brant George from *Folklore Forum* complimented the work by writing that it "stands as one of the few works available to non-Spanish speakers and readers which portrays with relative accuracy a Latin American tradition of oral narrator."[174]

The year 1970 was also momentous for another reason, because Paredes helped to found CMAS (The Center for Mexican American Studies) on The University of Texas at Austin campus. His two years as director were marked by both triumph and controversy. The program began with an enrollment of twenty-four students who became the embryo for one of the most successful Chicano Studies programs in the country.

In the late 1960s , the Chicano Student Movement at The University of Texas at Austin agitated for a Chicano Studies Center with a series of protests. When the president's office was occupied by students, Paredes soon became part of the cause as a type of mediator. José Limón, a member of that Chicano student group, remarked that Paredes and the students "were a type of bad cop and good cop. The students were the bad cop and Mr. Paredes was the good cop. Speaking the voice of reason to the university, Paredes said, '¿Qué vamos hacer con estos muchachos?' [What are we going to do with these boys?]"[175] Limón said that students jammed Paredes' office to speak to him. Some stood and some sat, but all worked on a concentrated strategy for the center. By 1970, the University had agreed to establish a center. A search was conducted for a director but was not successful because the director's required qualifications included that he or she be a full professor and there were few Mexican-American Ph.D.'s at the time. Paredes then agreed to take the job, believing that the center would provide courses related to the Chicano experience. He also requested that a second administrative position of assistant director be created for the program and that José Limón, a graduate assistant at the time, be given the post. The administration agreed to Paredes' request. The center soon began to develop and attract more students.

Paredes' tenure as director, however, was shortlived. A proposal was sent by the center personnel to the administration to develop a major in Mexican American studies. Some administrators seemed lukewarm about the project. They had clearly opposed the idea of a center from its inception. They would agree to the idea in principle only if the center was made part of the Latin America Studies Institute. Paredes vehemently opposed this. He sent a letter to the administration to that effect and received no response. After waiting for some time with no reply, he wrote another letter and was further frustrated when he was informed that his original proposal had been misplaced. Paredes became angry and wrote a letter of resignation. As a man of principle, he felt very insulted. However, his resignation created a crisis for the center by giving the administration an excuse to incorporate or dissolve it. Fortunately, that did not materialize and the center continued.[176]

For Paredes, the decade continued with the usual productivity and quality typical of his scholarship. Two of Paredes' articles published in 1970 were "Proverbs and Ethnic Stereotypes," which appeared in the *Proverbium* and "The Where and Why of Folklore," in *Illinois History*.

The following year, Paredes co-authored *The Urban Experience and Folk Tradition* with Ellen J. Stekert, which was published by The University of Texas Press. The work consists of a collection of essays combined into a special issue of the *Journal of American Folklore*. Products of a symposium held at Wayne State University in May 1968, the five essays are about diverse ethnic group traditions in urban areas. Paredes' comments about the essays make the work appealing to both folklorists and sociologists.

Also published in 1971 was an article in *25 Estudios de Folklore*, a book edited by Fernando Anaya Monroy. The article was entitled "Folklore e Historia: Dos Cantares de la frontera del Norte." The fact that it was published at the University of Americas in Mexico City was an indication that Paredes' international reputation was growing. A few months later, "The Hammon and the Beans" was reprinted in

The Chicano: From Caricature to Self-Portrait, edited by Edward Simmen. Paredes did not agree with Simmen's introduction which included a description of "a lazy bandit sleeping beneath the big sombrero in the shade of the adobe hut" who "has suddenly awakened."[177] He said that although that description was a widely held view of Mexicans, it was an erroneous one. For generations, Mexican Americans had been aware of their problems. "The Hammon and the Beans" story would reach many readers and would again be reprinted.

In 1972, Paredes co-authored two books. The first, entitled *Toward New Perspectives in Folklore,* was written with Richard Bauman. This book consists of essays including novel approaches for actually doing folklore investigations. In the foreword, Paredes explains the purpose of this endeavor:

> The North American folklorist, like many of his colleagues in the social sciences, has looked on theories less as the basis of sound methodologies and more as pronouncements with emotional, if not moral implication. He embraces them fervently when they appear, enshrining their proponents as prophets. Later, when experience shows that they will not answer all his questions, he denounces them in total, casts them into outer darkness, and begins all over again. Perhaps this is the reason meaningful dialogue has been scarce in our discipline.[178]

Included in the essays is information about developing viable and measurable research resulting in a type of folklore dialogue. The second book, co-authored with Raymund Paredes, was entitled *Mexican-American Authors.* In it was a section called "Dichos" or folksayings, which was the product of Paredes' extensive research on the topic.

This precedent-setting Chicano anthology examines the many varieties of Chicano literature. Its initial entry is the ballad of "Jacinto Treviño," acquired and translated by Paredes himself. Also included are brief narratives by Jovita Gónzalez, Roma native and former Brownsville resident. Mario Suarez, Josephina Niggli, Nick C. Vaca, Luis Omar Salinas, and Fermina Guerra were among the other contributing authors.

In 1973, Paredes was recognized by the Texas House of Representatives and given a Certificate of Citation for his service in preserving the border culture. In 1976, his article "The Role of Folklore in Border Relations," appeared in *San Diego/Tijuana—The International Border in Community Relations: Gateway or Barrier?*, a book edited by Kiki Skagen. Additionally, he published other articles including "El concepto de la 'médula emotiva' aplicado el corrido mexicano: Benjamín Argumedo" in *Folklore Americano*, "The United States, Mexico and Machismo" in the *Journal of the Folktale Institute*, and "José Mosqueda and the Folklorization of Actual Events," in *Aztlán: Chicano Journal of Social Science and the Arts*. "Folk Medicine and the Intercultural Jest" was reprinted in *Introduction to Chicano Studies* edited by Livie Isauro Durán and H. Russell Bernard. Paredes was also the series editor for *El Nacimiento del Niño Dios: A Pastorela from Tarimoro, Guanajuato* by Lily Litvak.

Paredes continued to speak at many functions, including graduation commencements. One such address was to the Crystal City High School graduating class of 1975. The message reflected what he had always believed. He said,

> The majority of you … I am sure … fall into the same category I found myself long ago. So there is really not much point in doing the same routine with you, about going out into the real world. You have been out there already, for a good length of time… However, there is a problem all people your age do face, no matter what your ethnic origins; and that is the problem of identity.[179]

If there were questions about Paredes' reputation as a nationally known scholar, they were answered with the publication of *A Texas-Mexican Cancionero: Folksongs of the Lower Border* (University of Illinois Press) in 1976. Undoubtedly, it is one of Paredes' most significant literary legacies because it expands the volume and preservation of the Mexican *corrido.*

In the introduction to *Cancionero,* Paredes explains what this compilation of songs represents, how long the songs have existed, and where they have traveled. Finally, he writes about the diversity and talent of men and women border ballad performers.

> The songs collected here are a people's heritage— their unselfconscious record of themselves, alien for the most part to documents and books. There are few enough writings about the Border people, who happen to be my people. The Anglos who came down to us as conquerors saw us as abysmal savages—benighted by papistry (priest-ridden, as that great Texas liberal, J. Frank Dobie, used to say) and debased by miscegenation (with ditchwater instead of blood in our veins, as another great Texas liberal and scholar, Walter Prescott Webb, once put it). The supercivilized intellectuals of the Mexican plateau were kinder to us; they merely knew us as los bárbaros del Norte, the barbarians of the North.
>
> The whole of a people's past is reflected in these songs, from the days when they journeyed out into Chichimecaland, mid-eighteenth century pioneers, traveling north until they reached the Río Grande, drank of its waters, and traveled no more. They settled on the river banks long before there was such a thing as the United States of America, and they struck roots that would last for centuries. They clustered around the river, for its waters were life. To these people, during their first century here, the river was the navel of the world.
>
> Then came the pale-eyed strangers from the north, and the homeland was divided. The river— once a focus of life—became a barrier, a dividing line,

an international boundary. Families and friends were artificially divided by it. For a long time, however, life went on very much as it had before. Officially, the people on one bank of the river were Mexicans; those on the other side were Americans, albeit an inferior, less-than-second-class type of American in the eyes of the new rulers of the land. But the inhabitants on both river banks continued to be the same people, with the same traditions, preserved in the same legends and the same songs. Together they entered into a century-long conflict with the English-speaking occupiers of their homeland. Time has changed things, as the governments from Washington and Mexico City have made their presence felt. Even so, the bonds reaching across the river have not been broken, just stretched out a bit to meet the demands of two forms of officialdom, originally disparate but growing more like each other day by day.[180]

The text is a robust compilation of sixty-six songs from five genres including their original lyrics and English translations. The five categories include "Old Songs from Colonial Days," "Songs of the Border Conflicts," "Songs for Special Occasions," "Romantic and Comic Songs," and "The Pocho Appears." Paredes began collecting these songs as a youth in Brownsville after hearing them performed by musicians on the ranchos.

In his introduction, Paredes wrote that the Río Grande had a magical effect on the colonists that came from Mexico and that the songs documented the Mexican American's lengthy struggle to maintain his identity and humanity. Also provided is information about song settings and the singers who left a lasting impression on Paredes. Additionally, Paredes provides insights into *frontera* celebrations and their dissemination of songs and legends. Each segment of the book is introduced with an essay conveying historical beginnings and tales associated with them.

To Paredes, cultural conflict was at the center of the border ballad. Many of these border corridos told stories about South Texas violence and the role that Anglos and Texas Rangers played in it. It was no surprise that the Mexicanos held the Anglos in contempt, and it was this theme that made these corridos unique. The rinches (Rangers) and Anglos are usually portrayed as untrustworthy. Corridos about border heros/ bandits such as Gregorio Cortez and Jacinto Treviño appear in the book. Jacinto Treviño, like the protagonist of Paredes' dissertation, Gregorio Cortez, is viewed as hero and outlaw. Because of altercations with the law in McAllen, Brownsville, and San Benito, Texas, Treviño is a wanted man. He challenges the rinches to capture him and calls them cowards as he returns to Mexico.[181] His deeds are chronicled in the following corrido.

Jacinto Treviño
    Ya con ésta van tres veces
que se ha visto lo bonito,
la primera fue en Macalen,
en Brónsvil, y en San Benito.

    Y en la cantina de Bekar
se agarraron a balazos,
por dondequiera saltaban
botellas hechas pedazos.

    Esa cantina de Bekar
al momento quedó sola,
nomás Jacinto Treviño
de carabina y pistola.

    - Entrenle, rinches cobardes,
que el pleito no es con un niño,
querían conocer su padre,
¡yo soy Jacinto Treviño!

- Entrenle, rinches cobardes,
validos de la ocasión,
no van a comer pan blanco
con tajadas de jamón. -

Decía el Rinche Mayor,
como era un americano:
- ¡Ah, qué Jacinto tan hombre,
no niega el ser mexicano! -

Decía Jacinto Treviño
que se moría de la risa:
- A mí me hacen los ojales,
los puños de la camisa. -

Decía Jacinto Treviño,
abrochándose un zapato:
- Aquí traigo más cartuchos
pa' divertirnos un rato. -

Decía Jacinto Treviño,
con su pistola en la mano:
- No corran, rinches cobardes,
con un solo mexicano. -

Decía Jacinto Treviño:
- Yo ya me vo' a retirar,
me voy para Río Grande
y allá los voy a esperar. -

Decía Jacinto Treviño,
al bajar una bajada:
- ¡Ay, qué rinches tan cobardes,
que no me haigan hecho nada! -

Decía Jacinto Treviño,
andando en Nuevo Laredo:
- Yo soy Jacinto Treviño,
nacido en Montemorelos. -

Ya con ésta me despido
aquí a presencia de todos,
yo soy Jacinto Treviño,
vecino de Matamoros.

Jacinto Treviño
(Translation)

With this it will be three times that beautiful things
    have been seen;
the first time was in McAllen, then in Brownsville,
    and San Benito.

They had a shoot-out at Baker's saloon;
broken bottles were popping all over the place.

Baker's saloon was immediately deserted;
only Jacinto Treviño remained, with his rifle and his
    pistol.

"Come on, you cowardly rinches, you're not playing
    games with a child.
You wanted to meet your father? I am Jacinto
    Treviño!

"Come on, you cowardly rinches, you always like to
    take the advantage;
this is not like eating white bread with slices of
    ham."

The chief of the rinches said, even though he was an
    American,
"Ah, what a brave man is Jacinto; you can see he is a
    Mexican!"

Then said Jacinto Treviño, who was dying of
    laughter,
"All you're good for is to make the buttonholes and
    the cuffs on my shirt."

Then said Jacinto Treviño, as he was tying his shoe,
"I have more cartridges here, so we can amuse our-
    selves a while."

Then said Jacinto Treviño, with his pistol in his hand,
"Don't run, you cowardly rinches, from a single
    Mexican."

Then said Jacinto Treviño, "I am going to retire.
I'm going to Río Grande City, and I will wait for you
    there."

Then said Jacinto Treviño, as he came down an
    incline,
"Ah, what a cowardly bunch of rinches; they didn't
    do anything to me!"

Then said Jacinto Treviño, when he was in Nuevo
    Laredo,
"I am Jacinto Treviño, born in Montemorelos."

Now with this I say farewell, here in everybody's
    presence;
I am Jacinto Treviño, a citizen of Matamoros.

One ballad, "Los Tequileros" is about the tequila runners of the Depression era, like those encountered by Paredes when he was a young newspaper delivery boy in Brownsville. Three "Tequileros" are killed by Texas Rangers and their ballad describes this tragedy.

El día dos de febrero,
qué día tan señalado!
mataron tres tequileros
los rinches del otro lado.

Llegaron al Río Grande,
se pusieron a pensar:
-Será bueno ver a Leandro
porque somos dos nomás. –

Le echan el envite a Leandro,
Leandro les dice que no:
-Fíjense que estoy enfermo,
así no quisiera yo. –

Al fin de tanto invitarle
Leandro los acompañó,
En las lomas del Almiramba
Fue el primero que murió.

Les hicieron un descargue
a mediación del camino,
cayó Gerónimo muerto,
Silvano muy mal herido.

Tumban el caballo a Leandro
y a él lo hirieron de un brazo,
ya no les podía hacer fuego,
tenía varios balazos.

La carga que ellos llevaban
era tequila anisado,
el rumbo que ellos llevaban
Era San Diego afamado.

Salieron desde Guerrero
con rumbo para el oriente,
allí les tenían sitiado
dos carros con mucha gente.

Cuando cruzaron el río
se fueron por un cañon,
se pusieron a hacer lumbre
sin ninguna precaución.

El capitán de los rinches
platicaba con esmero:
-Es bueno agarrar ventaja
Porque estos son de
Guerrero.-

Si los rinches fueran hombres
y sus caras presentaran,
entonce' a los tequileros
otro gallo nos cantara.

Pues ellos los tres murieron,
los versos aquí se acaban,
se les concedió a los rinches
las muertes que ellos deseaban.

El capitán de los rinches
a Silvano se acercó,
y en unos cuantos segundos
Silvano García murió.

Los rinches serán muy hombres,
no se les puede negar,
nos cazan como venados
para podernos matar.

El que compuso estos versos
no se hallaba allí presente,
estos versos son compuestos
por lo que decía la gente.

Aquí va la despedida
en medio de tres floreros,
y aquí se acaba el corrido,
versos de los tequileros.

The Tequila Runners (translation)
Note: This English translation includes several stanzas
not present in the Spanish version above. Rather, the
English version reprinted here includes stanzas from
several existing forms of the same corrido.

On the second day of February, what a memorable
    day!
The rinches from the other side of the river killed
    three tequila runners.

They reached the Río Grande and then they stopped
    and thought,
"We had better go see Leandro because there are
    only two of us."

They asked Leandro to go with them, and Leandro
    said he could not:
"I am sorry, but I'm sick. I don't want to go this way."

They kept asking him to go, until Leandro went with
    them;
in the hills of Almiramba, he was the first one to die.

The contraband they were taking was tequila anisado;
the direction they were taking was toward famed San
  Diego.

They left from Guerrero in an easterly direction;
two cars with many men were waiting for them there.

When they crossed the river, they traveled along a
  canyon;
Then they stopped and built a fire without any regard
  for danger.

The captain of the rinches was saying, speaking in
  measured tones,
"It is wise to stack the odds because these men are
  from Guerrero."

They fired a volley at them in the middle of the road;
Gerónimo fell dead and Silvano fell badly wounded.

They shot Leandro off his horse, wounding him in
  the arm.
He could no longer fire back at them; he had several
  bullet wounds.

The captain of the rinches came up to Silvano;
and in a few seconds, Silvano García was dead.

The rinches are very brave, there is no doubt of that;
the only way they can kill us is by hunting us like deer.

The soldiers of Tamaulipas handed him over to
  Nuevo León,
and as soon as they had reccived him, they killed him
  out of hand.

Because they were afraid of him, afraid he might be
    given some office,
they killed him on the road between Agualeguas and
    Cerralvo.

Your policemen of Guerrero, I have you all on my list;
you no longer will die of fright, because the Smuggler
    is dead.

Police of El Encinal, of San Fernando and Méndez,
now you can sleep soundly, for they have killed
    Reséndez.

God be with you, you policemen, and may Morpheus
    accompany you;
and so you won't get fright sickness, make it a custom
    to drink pennyroyal tea.

Now with this I say farewell, plucking a flower of May;
this is the end of the singing of the stanzas about Don
    Mariano.[182]

In 1977 Paredes wrote a book honoring the outstanding Texas
educator, George I. Sánchez. *Humanidad: Essays in Honor of George I.
Sanchez* was probably his most significant contribution to the field of
education. The volume covers a variety of subjects including Chicano history, bilingualism and biculturalism, and the Spanish language
in the Southwest. Additionally, Paredes included essays by intellectu-
als such as George I. Sánchez, Ricardo Flores Magón, Ernesto Galarza and the poet Justo Sierra. Sánchez was presented as a scholar, a
teacher, and an advocate of human rights who championed equal
educational opportunities for those who spoke Spanish and was ve-
hement about documenting the cultural bias of IQ tests. His work
resulted in the admission by some educators that test results for mi-
norities had indeed been misinterpreted.

That same year in the fall, Professor Paredes offered a graduate seminar course on Mariachi Music (Anthropology 394 M) for students in folklore and ethnomusicology. Décima, Corrido, Copla, and Related Forms was more than a course, however, because students enrolled for it, learned the music, and formed a mariachi ensemble. Among the variety of fundraisers created to support the new mariachi group was a bake sale held at the West Mall of The University of Texas at Austin on November 19, 1977. Amelia, Américo's wife, was involved in the baking and the sale.[183]

Officially, "El Mariachi Paredes de Tejastitlán" was comprised of eleven persons, men and women, Anglo and Mexican-Americans. It performed five times in early February 1978, at the international Charro Days festival in Brownsville, Texas. Regrettably because of ill health, Paredes was unable to attend. During the spring semester, Paredes designated his close friend Dr. Gérard Béhague from the Department of Music as faculty advisor.[184]

The Mariachi Paredes de Tejastitlán was the first university-based performing group of its kind in Texas. The Department of Music and the Center for Intercultural Studies in Folklore and Ethnomusicology co-sponsored the group. The group not only originated with Paredes but was named in his honor at a private performance for the Society of Ethnomusicology in early November 1977. One of the musicians in the mariachi group was Manuel Peña, a Valleyite from Mission, Texas. He later became a professor, music scholar, and author in Texas and California.

Two years later, José Limón, Dr. Paredes' former student and colleague, wrote the following words about his colleague and former professor,

> Américo Paredes is first and foremost a product of his land. He thoroughly enjoys drinking "una helada," (a cold beer) and he loves engaging in the humorous exchanges so typical of the Mexican border country. Occasionally he can even be persuaded to take out

his guitar and sing a few of the region's old songs.
He knows of his influence among his own people.
He is gratified to know that students of Mexican descent come long distances to study with him. But he
remains a modest and unassuming man. Great men
are often like that.[185]

In 1978, Paredes initiated "Taco Seminars" with Chicano Students
on the UT campus. These seminars brought educational, economic,
and political issues affecting Chicanos to a public venue.

For Américo Paredes, the decade of the 1970s ended with local, national, and international recognition for over twenty years of
scholarship and teaching. In 1977, Paredes was elected to the North
American Academy of the Spanish Language with corresponding
membership in the Spanish Royal Academy. In 1978, he received the
Outstanding Faculty Award from The University of Texas Minority
Student Services and in 1979, Paredes was awarded the Austin Chapter of the American GI Forum award for his continuous educational
contributions. The same year he received a citation for contributions
to Hispanic scholarship in the Humanities from the Congressional
Hispanic Caucus and National Endowment for the Humanities. Additionally, the Texas Association of Chicanos in Higher Education
established the Américo Paredes Award as an annual award to young
Chicano scholars.

In September 1980, Américo Paredes celebrated his sixty-fifth
birthday. On campus, his students and colleagues honored him with
a birthday party and celebrated his contributions. A few months earlier in Houston, the National Association for Chicano Studies, since
renamed National Association for Chicana and Chicano Studies,
dedicated its Eighth Annual Conference to Paredes.

For two decades, Don Américo had served his students and his
university well, yet there was still much to be done. At the beginning of the new decade, retirement was far from his mind. However,
events in the 1980s occurred that were beyond his control and would
ultimately lead to changes.

Through the decade Paredes communicated with Chicano leaders such as Alurista.

Although the quantity of scholarship declined for Paredes during the 1980s, the quality did not. In an article for the *Illinois Folklore* journal, Paredes explained that folklore was no longer only the knowledge (lore) of an ethnic group (folk) tribe or people. He said, "Our view nowadays is that almost any 'special group' may have its own folklore, in simplest terms, a 'special group' is identified as an aggregation of persons who think of themselves as a unit and as being somewhat different from the crowd for one reason or another."[186] He attributed the current interest to four reasons: 1) the shifting of folklore studies from the sole consideration of survival to the concept of folklore and human behavior, 2) the need to secure national identity in a rapidly changing and confusing world, 3) the creation of small group identity in a larger society which makes us anonymous and 4) the contemporary folklore research which deals with today's problems.[187] Many years later in an article in *Aztlán*, Paredes described folklore as "the unofficial heritage of a people," significant to minority groups, especially those whose language was different from those in the majority. For Mexican Americans, folklore was important because "their basic sense of identity is expressed in a language"[188] with no official status.

In 1982, *Aztlán: International Journal of Chicano Studies Research* published a Paredes article entitled "Folklore, Lo Mexicano and Proverbs." One year later Paredes participated in the Second Symposium of Mexican and United States Universities on Border Studies. His essay entitled "The Corrido: Yesterday and Today" was selected as the honor essay and subsequently published in the proceedings. Also in 1983, Paredes published "Nearby Placcs and Strange-Sounding Names" in an anthology entitled *The Texas Literary Tradition: Fiction, Folklore, History* edited by Don Graham and others. In 1987, the Stanford Center for Chicano Research published Paredes' essay for the Inaugural Ernesto Galarza Commemorative Lecture. It was entitled "The Undying Love of 'El Indio' Córdova: Décimas and Oral

History in a Border Family." After thirty years, Paredes continued to increase the significant amount of research about décimas that he had begun years earlier.

Early in the decade, Paredes had received the prestigious Ashbel Smith Professorship, a recognition of his scholarship and teaching of folklore theory, American literature, and Latin American and Mexican folklore.[189] This award had been authorized by the Board of Regents to recognize ten professors at UT-Austin for academic excellence. In 1982 he received a plaque of recognition from the university for twenty-five years of contributions to Mexican and Mexican American culture and another plaque from the National Association of Mexican Universities for his diffusion of Mexican culture in the United States. He was also honored at the Primera Mesa Redonda de Folklore y Etnomusicología in Zamora, Michoacán, Mexico.

That year on June 29, public television's "American Playhouse" series aired *The Ballad of Gregorio Cortez*, directed by Robert M. Young. It starred Edward James Olmos as Cortez. Olmos had previously appeared in *Zoot Suit*. Generally, the historical movie received favorable reviews. Charles Champlin from the *Los Angeles Times* called it "a smashing chase Western—the loner having escaped a lynching and massacre … eluding the followers until he will flee no more and fatalistically, apparently elects to take his chances on Anglo justice."[190] John O'Connor commented that "the film adopts, quite successfully, the almost stately pacing of a long ballad, of a myth in the making." Olmos's performance was described as "superior."[191] Paredes' own comments, however, were not as generous. In June 1982, he wrote to a friend, Carolyn Osborn, about the film. "As a movie, it is a good job, with most of the credit going to Robert Young, the director, who rewrote a trite script by Víctor Villaseñor … The thing that bothered me most, though, was Eddie Olmos' interpretation of Cortez. He took a character noted for his coolness, dignity, and courage and turned him into a scared little peón, a kind of Tex-Mex Charlie Chaplin. I'm disgusted with him, especially because he could have done it differently if he had wanted to. He's a good actor. Those details aside, it is a good movie—outstanding photography, too."[192] Years later, Paredes was even more candid about the movie. He said, "You have life completely reproducing tradition [in the ballad]. Because what oral tradition says is that he [Cortez] was a peaceful man. He rose in wrath. That's why I hate this garbage that was put out as a movie."[193] The television film premiered at Bates Hall. His family and his colleagues, including Rolando Hinojosa, attended.

Paredes periodically returned to his hometown of Brownsville to visit relatives or to speak at various functions. He spoke on two occasions at commencement at his junior college alma mater, Texas Southmost College. In 1982, he spoke to the graduating class about "undergoing graduation" and the rite of passage. He said, "It is interesting that, among many cultures, rites of passage are symbolical by gateways or doors, through which the individual passes in reaching a new stage in his or her journey through life ... In this context, graduation is a special rite of coming of age."[194] In his closing statement, he said that Anglos and Mexicans alike "are aware that overriding political considerations, there are cultural and economic factors ruling our lives that make us all one, that our destinies are intertwined regardless of our ethnic origins."[195]

In 1983, he was awarded the Dickson, Allen, Anderson Centennial Professorship in Southwest Folklore, History, and Literature, the first professor in his discipline to be honored, and in 1985, he was named Honorary Member of The Western Literature Association. In 1987, Paredes was recognized with the Américo Paredes Distinguished Lecture Series established by The University of Texas at Austin. Professor Luis Leal from the University of California-Santa Barbara presented the first lecture. The lecture series continues today and is held annually in the first week of May. In 1989, Paredes was awarded the Charles Frankel Prize by the National Endowment for the Humanities, an award for a lifetime devoted to scholarship in the humanities. Here, too, he became the first Mexican American to receive the honor.

By the mid-1980s, the life of Américo Paredes had changed dramatically due to a series of life-threatening illnesses. His failing health and the death of his brother and friend, Amador, would change some of his focus from scholarship to family and personal matters.

On September 26, 1984, Paredes had surgery to remove a cancerous testicle. By this time, Amador had already become ill. Américo's indomitable humor remained intact as he explained his symptoms in a letter to his closest brother. He described the bloody discharge that he had to endure and the bother it produced. But despite the discomfort, Paredes assured Amador that his condition would soon improve and that he would visit him in Brownsville. Américo also felt sorry for Nena, his wife, who was taking care of him and her eighty-three-year-old mother, who had recently suffered a fall. Despite his condition, Paredes wrote a few personal off-color lines to humor his ailing brother: "You have probably heard of the famous Chinese gentleman, Wan Hung Lo. I am now acquainted with a Mexican Vietnamese by the name of Juan Dong On. Sorry looking guy, he is."[196]

Five years after Américo's death, Alan Paredes commented that his father was greatly affected by Amador's death in 1984 from colon cancer. He was depressed for several months. "I think that if my Uncle Amador hadn't died, my father would not have retired when he did."[197] Ricardo Romo, then associate provost at The University of Texas at Austin, helped him. Alan recalls Romo saying that "Américo would come once a week to his office at the University."[198] This was probably therapeutic for him.

Although Paredes retired from full-time teaching in 1984, he continued to teach part-time for the next few years. The one class that he did teach, however, was filled with students who admired and respected the man who had done so much for his generation and for theirs.

Paredes now turned much of his attention to writing. The result was the publication of five books. Arte Público Press published *George Washington Gómez: A Mexicotexan Novel* (1990), *Between Two Worlds*

(1991), *Uncle Remus con chile* (1993), *The Hammon and the Beans and Other Stories* (1994), and *The Shadow* (1998). The University of Texas Center for Mexican American Studies published *Folklore and Culture on the Texas-Mexican Border* (1993).

George Washington Gómez: A Mexicotexan Novel appeared fifty years after Américo Paredes had nearly completed it. It has been described as his "most outstanding contribution to Chicano fiction."[199] Rolando Hinojosa, Tejano writer and a former colleague of Paredes, describes the novel as "a work set against the Great Depression, the onset of World War II in Europe, and set also against the over 100-year-old conflict of cultures in the Lower Río Grande Valley of Texas..."[200]

The novel is divided into five sections: Los Sediciosos (The Seditionists), Jonesville-on-the-Grande, Dear Old Gringo School Days, La Chilla (The Squeal), and Leader of His People. In "Los Sediciosos" Paredes introduces the main character, Guálinto, named after George Washington, but pronounced Guálinto by his grandmother and his father, Gumercindo, who is an innocent victim of murder by the Texas Rangers. Gumercindo was believed to be linked to the South Texas seditionist movement led by Anacleto de la Peña and Guálinto's uncle, Lupe García. Because of the violence along the border, Tejanos and Mexicanos lived in fear.

In the Jonesville-on-the-Grande section, Guálinto's mother, María, moves to Jonesville, protected by her brother Feliciano. She, Guálinto, and his two sisters, Maruca and Carmen, now live in a city that was founded after the U.S.-Mexican War. It soon becomes evident that the environment in Jonesville is violent. Sometimes Guálinto plays games that mirror real life when he pretends to kill rinches while stabbing banana stalks in the quiet backyard of his home. He concludes that rinches can easily kill Mexicans, so he must kill rinches when he becomes a man. While the Mexican Revolution is raging in Mexico, Feliciano, his uncle, wages his war against Anglos. He tells Guálinto that this family lost much of its land years ago. Angrily, he tells the boy that the gringos took it and it became part of the King Ranch.

"Dear Old Gringo School Days" depicts a school system that has a double standard, one for Anglos and one for Mexican Americans. The prejudice against the Mexican American children is in the tracking of those children in the lowest classes of the first and second grades until they learn English. Only then can they attend regular classes. Guálinto is highly intelligent and represents the future of the family. Guálinto, however, is also victimized in school and out of school. In school he is humiliated by being between beaten and publicly embarrassed for having written a love note to a girl. Out of school, he is not allowed to attend a high school party at a nightclub because the establishment does not admit Mexican Americans. These experiences make it very difficult for Guálinto to be the great man and leader of his people that his father had wished him to be.

In the section "La Chilla," Guálinto, now eighteen years old, encounters hope and suffering. He hopes to write a timeless poem for his childhood sweetheart, María Elena Osuna. Yet Guálinto faces the effects of the Great Depression. During these years Mexicans were "repatriated" from many parts of the United States, including the Midwest and the Southwest, to Mexico to alleviate the cost of their presence in the United States. Guálinto is a U.S. citizen but he suffers wage discrimination when he does find employment. The phrase "La Chilla" is used by the characters to describe the minimal value that Anglo authorities place on Mexican lives. "Sugar is two cents a pound and men are two cents a dozen, Mexicans half-price. Flour costs a quarter a sack, a quarter costs all of a man's efforts and the little pride he has left. La Chilla."[201]

Guálinto, however, faces other challenges. His sister, Maruca, becomes pregnant and not only dishonors and shames her family, but almost causes its disintegration. To add to his anguish, Guálinto encounters a wanted man who threatens him with a gun. During the struggle, Guálinto hits him with a brick. The injured man, Lupe García, who had changed his name to Arnulfo Miranda, eventually dies of pneumonia. Guálinto discovers that García was a fugitive because he had killed the Texas Ranger who had killed Guálinto's father. Guálinto is taken to the police station, asked some questions and then has coffee with the chief of police. He is then told that he will receive a reward.

The fifth and final section of the book concludes with a touch of irony. By the late 1930s, Guálinto has grown, become a lawyer in Washington, D.C., and changed his name to George G. Gómez. He returns to Jonesville-on-the-Grande before the United States enters World War II. By his side is an Anglo wife named Ellen Dell. He enters the military and becomes a first lieutenant working counter-intelligence for the U.S Army. He returns to Jonesville from Washington, D.C. to investigate the possibility of border sabotage by the Germans. Guálinto has assimilated into the Anglo culture and has become a *vendido* (sellout). His faith in his people has all but disappeared along with his loyalty to his culture and heritage.

The novel was written when the Río Grande Valley was experiencing dramatic changes. The railroad that had come to the Valley in the early 1900s had provided a reliable and efficient mode of transportation for people and farm goods, but the railroad tracks often segregated Anglos and Mexican Americans in most Valley cities. The effects of the Mexican Revolution were being felt in deep South Texas with episodes of guerrilla warfare. For example, in Olmito a train was attacked and derailed. The Texas Rangers often "persuaded" rancheros to sell their land and the Great Depression was affecting many people in the area. Paredes lived the era of Jonesville-on-the-Grande. Guálinto and the Rinches are modeled on people in the Brownville that he grew up with.

In 1991, Américo Paredes completed another work that he had begun over five decades earlier. *Between Two Worlds* includes poems written as early as the 1930s. Some are from his original *Cantos de Adolescencia*, some are from his World War II and post-war experiences, and some are more recent works. A few of his poems had previously appeared in Texas newspapers. He wrote many of his poems on bits of paper. In 1960, he went to Boca Chica Beach and burned many of his poems. Some of those that were not burned, however, became part of *Between Two Worlds*. Paredes said,

> On September 3, 1960, I attained the age of forty-five and what I judged was a mature and stable state of mind; so I decided it was time to destroy the fruits of my labors in what, with a good deal of poetic license, might be called poetry. These had been piling up in varied envelopes and manila folders for more than thirty years. Some of them, done in Spanish mostly, had already been set loose upon the world in various publications. Palo dado ni Dios lo quita. But most of them were at hand in yellowing pieces of paper of all shapes and sizes. In the ensuing months I did destroy a goodly number of them, those that were so painfully bad I could not bear to look at them twice. But I never got around to consigning all of them to the flames. For one thing, I was convinced that a dozen or so were worth saving, though I never could decide which dozen or so they might be. For another, all the survivors had personal value for me, whatever their lack of literary merit. So I put off the holocaust until I too should be closer to cremation. In the years that followed I even added a few more to the pile.[202]

The book consists of two major sections. Section one contains eighty-four poems, some in English and some in Spanish. The initial poem, "The Río Grande," originally written in 1934, is the English version of the poem that appeared in *Cantos de Adolescencia* entitled "El Río Bravo." Paredes searched for comfort and calm in the river, yet believes that the river is also tortured. The poem reflects the theme of the volume.

Throughout this book, Paredes describes his struggle with his soul and the challenges of duality between two worlds. Other poems in this first section discuss themes about his Mexican American identity, man's universal pain, and the impact of diverse cultural forces on people. "Ahí no más" (There, no more) presents the New World indigenous people as both a source of inner and physical strength and a significant part of his Chicano heritage. As Paredes describes, the indigenous people are his "Indian dark brother from whose ancestors half of father's fathers sprang."[203] Paredes also includes poems about his World War II experiences including his travels to China, Manchuria, and Japan. Love poetry and humorous verses about army personnel and the military constitute the remainder of the selections.

The second section, "From Cantos a Carolina 1934–1946" of *Between Two Worlds* includes ten lyric poems with themes about nature, beauty, and love. Several of these are intimate thoughts of a young man in love with a beautiful green-eyed woman who is in his dreams and in his heart.[204]

V.	V.
Ojos mareños,	Eyes of the ocean
ojos de luz,	Eyes of light
ojos risueños	Eyes of laughter
de verde azul,	Of blue-green
En tus pupilas	In your pupils
llenas de amor	Full of love
bebió el cariño	Drank the affection
que en mi nació	That in me was born
Ojos tristes	Saddened eyes
Soñadores	Dreamy eyes
Yo también soñé de amores	I too dreamed of love
Yo también	I too [205]

At the end of the book in the section entitled "Notes and Random Comments," Paredes writes that some of his verses were first published in *The Valley Morning Star*, a Harlingen-based newspaper, *La Prensa*, the San Antonio-based newspaper, *El Regional*, a Matamoros-based newspaper, and the *South Review*. Also included are specific comments about poem titles and insight into his poetry.

Paredes was once again published as a folklorist with his *Uncle Remus con chile* in 1993. The book contains 217 folk texts collected in Spanish and in English. The fieldwork for this collection was done throughout the 1960s and early '70s in deep South Texas, northern and central Mexico, and in the American Midwest. The texts are viable interlingual materials with many of the stories in Spanish with English punch lines. Others are humorous jests about difficult issues such as ethnic discrimination. Paredes is meticulous in providing not only background information on interviewees, but also pertinent notes and bibliographical information.

Anglo tourists and interethnic conflict between Anglos and Mexican Americans are two major themes of this book. Jokes are also made about the Texas Rangers and even historical figures such as Antonio López de Santa Anna. For example, "Los Vendidos por Santa Anna (#56)" tells a brief story about how Santa Anna sold the northern territory of Mexico rather than allow Mexican ranchers (rancheros) and cowboys (vaqueros) to defend their land against the United States. As a result, Mexicans call Mexican Americans "los vendidos por Santa Anna"[206] because they were lost with the territory.

A common thread for other jokes is racism. In "Dogs Allowed (#7)," Paredes explains that a small town in Central Texas had a sign reading "No Dogs or Mexicans Allowed." Further down the street was another restaurant run by Mexicans. Its sign read "Dogs Allowed, Gringos Too."[207] Another humorous text about racial discrimination is a response to an educational survey about discriminatory practices in South Texas schools. One particular question asked whether there were discrimination practices. The Río Grande City superintendent of schools replied, "There is no discrimination down here. We treat Anglos just like everybody else."[208]

Some are about the use of English and Spanish along the border. The following serve as two examples:

Talking American (#21)

I was going to A&M, you know, and I came home on vacation. I rode back with an Anglo from the Valley who was also coming back. On the way we got to talking, and the Anglo was arguing that us people down here ought to stop talking "Mexican." After all, we live in the United States. Why not talk American?

Well, we stop to have a beer on the road, in one of those little central Texas towns. All the people around us at the bar are talking German. So I poke my friend in the ribs. "Is that Mexican they're talking? Sure doesn't sound like American to me."

Frijoles y cabritos (#21)

It was two Anglos that had just come out of a conversational Spanish class, and one of them asked the other, "Have you learned—. What have you learned in the class you're taking?"

He says, "Oh, I learned a good one today," he says. "I'm really advancing in my Spanish."

"Well, say something."

"Well, let's see… ah… Oh, yeah, here it is. 'Dónde frijol, cabrito?'"

"I don't seem to—. What do you mean by that?"

"Where you been, kid?"[209]

The Center for Mexican American Studies published yet another of Paredes' books, *Folklore and Culture on the Texas-Mexican Border,* in 1993, the same year as *Uncle Remus*. It contains eleven of his most memorable essays, previously published between 1958 and 1987. The two sections of the book are entitled "The Social Base and the Negotiation of Identity" and "The Folklore Genres: History, Form and Performance."

Richard Bauman introduced the book with insightful comments on Paredes:

> Paredes writes not only in different languages but also in multiple voices. His scholarship is a richly textured expressive fabric, not at all confined to the standard expository prose and the we-they oppositions of conventional folkloric and anthropological scholarship. There is, to be sure, a fair share of expository prose in Paredes's writings, but it is a prose whose seriousness is constantly tempered by irony, Paredes's favorite critical trope, his own intercultural jest that simultaneously employs the discourse of mainstream scholarship and subverts it. Then, too the expository prose alternates in Paredes's scholarly writings with dedicatory lyric poems, recollections of personal experiences, songs from his own repertoire, legends recast and retold from the tellings of others, and other styles and genres. As for we-the oppositions, there are certainly plenty in Paredes's work, including we the scholars and they the Texas-Mexicans, but often Paredes crosses the border, and it is we the Texas-Mexicans against the Anglo scholars.
>
> Which is all to say, in the end, that there is a deep and resonant unity in Américo Paredes's life, his subject, and his writing, but it is a unity of diversity, a conjunction of the borders. And when you can balance the ambiguities, survive the conflict, and command the resources and repertoires of both sides of the border and the contact culture itself, as Américo Paredes has done, the result is inspired and inspiring writing.[210]

The first essay in the book, "The Folklore of Groups of Mexican Origin in the United States," was published in 1979 and is a milestone addition to folklore in the United States. Here, Paredes writes that intercultural conflict is the basis for Mexican American folklore. Paredes presents as early examples Gregorio Cortez, Elfego Baca, Aniceto Pizaña, and Juan Cortina, all bandit/hero figures. They were the subjects of ballads or corridos that became timeless along the border and led to the writing of other ballads.

In essay ten, entitled "The Décima on the Texas-Mexican Border: Folksong as an Adjunct to Legend," Paredes emphasizes that "the décima for centuries has been an important folksong type among all people of Spanish culture... It is more likely that it was developed by court poets and later taken up by the folk. Whatever the origins of the décima in Spain, it is clear that its diffusion in Spanish America came through cultivated sources."[211]

In "On Ethnographic Work Among Minority Groups: A Folklorist's Perspective," the fourth essay, he examines the feud between Chicano and Anglo anthropologists. Paredes asserts that the portrayal of Mexicans and Chicanos in many anthropological studies is unrealistic and that ethnographers who study minority groups in the United States must implement more stringent methods to obtain valid findings. In this collection, Paredes cautions ethnographers that not learning the language of their subjects can cause them to misinterpret comments. Those, in turn, may lead to inaccurate generalizations. This is especially true when dealing with colloquialisms.[212] Paredes' perspective on border folklore and Chicano ethnography can be much better comprehended with an understanding of the essays in *Folklore and Culture*.

The Hammon and the Beans and Other Stories, published in 1994, consists of seventeen short stories and adds yet another Paredes contribution to Chicano literature. Several of the stories are set in the Valley in Jonesville-on-the-Grande as was *George Washington Gómez*. This and the presence of Fort Jones, of course, represent the Brownsville and Fort Brown that Paredes remembered from his youth. Other stories are set during World War II in the Pacific theater. In "A Cold Night," a boy is witness to a murder and fears death. He is distressed about his feelings, curses God for what has happened, and seeks reassurance from the Virgen de Guadalupe.[213] "The Gringo" is a glimpse of a historical romance, which takes place at the onset of the U.S.-Mexican War in 1846. Ygnacio, the "gringo" of the story, is mistaken for such because of his blue eyes and fair skin. His father and brothers were killed, but he is not because he looked white. His wounds, however, required care. Prudence, the daughter of one of the men who shot Ygnacio and killed his family, tends his wounds, attempts to teach him English, and tries to Christianize him. When the father suspects a budding romance and sees Ygnacio as just another "greaser," Ygnacio is forced to flee. He is later killed by an American officer at the Battle of Palo Alto.[214]

Ramón Saldívar comments in the introduction of *The Hammon and the Beans* about Paredes' book:

> In all the stories collected here... the guiding force of that narrator is ironic wisdom. Paredes' border subjects acknowledge the social dimension of differences. Repeatedly, this acknowledgment occurs aesthetically in the shapes and nuances of a variety of oral forms, gestures, expressions and styles, that is, in the formulaic patterns that disguise and sometimes reveal humanity. The new, Pan-American history that he narrates traverses imaginary border lines and immigration checkpoints to document the imaginative styles concerned with Mexican American struggles for social justice.[215]

The recognition at all levels continued during the last decade of his life. In 1990, Paredes received La Orden del Águila Azteca, the Order of the Aztec Eagle, from the Mexican government. Bernice Rendón Talavares, former Mexican consul of Brownsville, stated, "The Mexican Order of the Aztec Eagle is a distinction presented by the Mexican government to foreigners with the objective of recognizing their prominent service to Mexico or to humanity. It corresponds by courtesy, with some exceptions to foreign dignitaries."[216]

Paredes' lifetime of work preserving both border culture and human rights was now recognized with the most prestigious award given by Mexico to a non-Mexican. He was unable to attend the presentation ceremony in Mexico City, but a special presentation was held at the Flawn Academic Center at The University of Texas at Austin. David Montejano, noted Chicano historian and a friend of Paredes at the university, wrote,

> I should note that Don Américo was equally unforgiving of the "cowardly" behavior of Mexicans and Mexican Americans in the face of racism. I recall his acceptance ... He launched into a biting critique of Mexican intellectuals who had ridiculed the "low culture" of Texas Mexicans, and who had impassively stood by during the outrages of Jim Crow segregation. It was an incredible performance; it is burned into my memory "pa' siempre."[217]

Paredes was graceful in receiving the honor, but truthful about how he felt when Mexican scholars at times did not take the scholarship of their Mexican-American counterparts seriously enough. Bluntly, he said, "for a long time, Mexican Americans have been objects of scorn and discrimination by both Mexicans and Anglo-Americans." He pointed out that in the United States, Mexican Americans had met their citizenship obligations in four major wars and had done so with dignity and courage. He ended by indicating that the relationship between the United States, Mexico, and Mexican Americans was improving.[218]

Paredes became the third professor from The University of Texas to receive the prestigious award. Nettie Lee Benson and Stanley Ross were earlier recipients. Other notable recipients of Mexican descent that year were César Chávez, founder of the United Farm Workers and civil rights leader, and Julián Zamora, the long-time professor of sociology at Notre Dame.[219] Mexico again recognized Paredes in 1991 with La Orden de José de Escandón. This honor, named after the Spanish colonizer of the mid-eighteenth century, recognized Paredes' prolific research about the border and in particular his work on the northern Mexico frontier.

In October 1993, The University of Texas at Austin recognized the lengthy contribution of Paredes to the institution by hosting "Regional Identity and Cultural Tradition: The Tejano Contribution, A Symposium in Honor of Don Américo Paredes." In 1995, Paredes was selected as a Distinguished Alumnus from what was now The University of Texas at Brownsville. Initially he declined because of his health, but university officials traveled to Austin and convinced him to reconsider. Because he was too ill to attend the commencement ceremonies, he was videotaped in Austin. The tape was shown outdoors on a large screen to the graduates in May. On the tape, Paredes said that he could not attend a university in Brownsville after graduating from Texas Southmost College in 1936 because there was none. He remarked,

> Now things have come around full circle. The university I could not attend in 1936 is now in my hometown, Brownsville. So this is a special occasion for me... So should I tell you young graduates how beautiful your future looks? How easy things will be for you because of the gains achieved by earlier generations? No I will not tell you that. Times are changing, we are told, and we can only hope that the change ultimately will be for the better.[220]

In 1997 Paredes received yet another recognition from his alma mater in Austin. That year he was awarded The University of Texas Presidential Citation for his significant studies during the 1940s and 1950s concerning the lower Texas border. These studies were nothing less than inspirational to an emerging generation of Mexican American scholars.

On November 14, 1998, Paredes and Texas author A. C. Greene received lifetime achievement awards from the Texas legislature at the State Capitol. Future First Lady Laura Bush presented them with the awards during the opening ceremonies of the Texas Book

Festival. UT-Austin Professor Rolando Hinojosa addressed Paredes'
literary contributions and singer Tish Hinojosa performed her music, including "Con Su Pluma en Su Mano," (With His Pen in His
Hand) during the tribute.[221]

Ten days later, Paredes was again honored by his hometown and
his Brownsville alma mater, The University of Texas at Brownsville-
Texas Southmost College. Among those who made remarks at the
tribute were UTB/TSC President Dr. Juliet V. García, Federal Judge
Reynaldo G. Garza, long-time friend Bruce Aiken, and Américo's
niece, Margot Torres, whose comments were moving and personal: "As a child I fondly remember my mother reciting décimas and
when I'd ask who had written them, she'd respond, 'tu tío Américo.'
She holds dearly to these poems and décimas as if many of the words
were her own. My mother says he would do great things..."[222]

At the end of the tribute, Paredes needed assistance getting to
the podium, due to previous illnesses and his age. Still strong in spirit, however, Américo spoke about the past and the future, his generation, and the generation of young people in the audience.

> I am extremely honored not only because of all you
> have done for me but how much you who are here
> represent. Our story has been one that has taken
> some time. Don Carlos Castañeda was the first one
> at The University of Texas at Austin. His sister was my
> primary school teacher, Miss Josephine, so I know a
> great deal about them... Don Carlos Castañeda was
> better known in Spain and other places than he was
> known at The University of Texas at Austin at that
> time. So, I see him as a step forward. When I think
> also about what we have done since... I think of it
> more as a slope we're moving up. Now the thing is
> for you young ones to keep pushing up. If you stop,
> you'll roll to the bottom again. So, I think I come at
> the tail end of a proud tradition... I hope and I know
> that you will continue with that tradition. I think that

is about all that I have to say except to say how many times can I say thank you. I could say it all day in the few languages that I know. I still would not really fulfill or explain the gratitude and the honor for what you have done for me.[223]

Dr. Paredes was staying with his family at South Padre Island during Thanksgiving week as he had done many times before. I had the privilege of bringing him to the tribute and driving him back to the island. Both the tribute during the morning and the concert that evening were attended by overflowing crowds. After the morning ceremonies, he held a book signing. Américo, although frail, signed every book with the respect that people continued to admire in him.

That night on the return trip to the island we stopped in Port Isabel. He said that he wanted to buy some Church's chicken and then asked me if I would join him for a beer and some chicken. As I drove home on that cool and breezy November evening, I contemplated the day's activities and what they might have meant to the hundreds who came to honor him and to Américo who was being proudly remembered by his hometown. Time seemed to stand still for the two of us. It was the last time I would see him alive.

Américo and his family returned to Austin. His health steadily declined for the next few months and soon he developed pneumonia. The last two months of his life Paredes spent at Specialty Hospital in Austin. On May 5, 1999, he died with family and friends around him. Even during his last days, Don Américo was the consummate educator. He was impatient to go home and periodically would attempt to sit up in the bed. His voice was very weak. Manfred del Castillo, one of his nephews from Brownsville remembers, "He wanted to get up; he wanted to get up, and Vince, his son who's got a Ph.D. in music, I believe, said, 'dad, dad, lay down, lay down,' Américo struggled and he said, 'it's _lie_ down, _lie_ down'... Even to the last breath, he was a teacher."[224]

On the day their father died, Alan and Vince noticed that their mother had developed jaundice. The next week they took her to the doctor. He informed her that she had pancreatic cancer, and it was terminal. When she asked him how long she had to live, he replied that she had from two weeks to three months. She lived three months. Her pancreatic cancer had spread to her liver.[225] In what seemed a blink of an eye, Américo and Nena were both gone.

Américo had written in his unpublished "Old Notes" of the 1930s:

> And the seconds tick away into hours, the hours into years. Time glides by like a fox, scarcely seeming to move, yet traveling at a lightning pace. And I am standing still. Each minute throws a silk-like thread around me, tying me down more firmly to the place where, Gulliver-like, I sprawl. It is futile that I strain at my bonds, so tenuous yet so strong. It is useless that I fret against the inevitable.
>
> But I do. I know that these scraps must die with me because I shall never have time to give them autonomous life. For I cannot withhold the march of time. I cannot live forever. I know that every moment, I am living I am also dying. I know that I shall pass from the world as passes a boat over the waters, scarcely stirring the waves by its passing.
>
> And these thoughts do but hasten my end.[226]

What could be more befitting for the passing of a Chicano hero? Américo Paredes was born during the height of the Mexican Revolution and died on Cinco de Mayo, 1999. He could not have orchestrated his passing any better. His family complied with his last wishes: cremation and a private funeral in Austin, Texas. A special tribute was published by The Center for Mexican American Studies shortly after his death. Deborah Kapchan, director of the Center for Intercultural Studies on Folklore and Ethnomusicology at UT-Austin, wrote of his legacy to her.

> Some people influence us so subtly that we barely notice, like a taste that permeates our palate we do not

recognize it. Until it is absent; and then the world "tastes" different, the salt somehow missing. This is how Dr. Paredes's scholarship affected me—so much a part of my folklore education that it formed a part of its essential flavor. I first encountered Dr. Paredes's work as a graduate student in folklore at the University of Pennsylvania. Dr. Paredes's writings on borderland folklore genres embodied clarity without sacrificing complexity, integrating humor into a history of oppression that needed telling. When I found myself teaching at The University of Texas I explored his legacy in more depth; later, directing the Folklore Center that Dr. Paredes founded in 1967, I felt a responsibility for its transmission.

Although I did not spend much time with Dr. Paredes, his presence at the center—both physical when he visited Frances Terry on Tuesdays, and spiritual (the spirit of his writing)—was a source of great inspiration, the gentle humility of his person a reminder that true talent and dedication are not accompanied by arrogance. Dr. Paredes was a poet, sensitive to the injustices of life, but unwilling to be embittered by them. His oeuvre stands as a testimony to the power of beauty—the beauty of the corrido, the décima, the copla, the beauty of his writings on these genres as well as his own creative writings—to defy the forces in life that would have us despair.[227]

Rolando Hinojosa, Ellen Clayton Garwood Professor in Creative Writing in the English Department at UT-Austin, wrote about his fond memories of Paredes.

I first heard of Américo during my teenage years through my late brother-in-law, O. B. García, who gave me the original *Brownsville Herald* copy of "The Mexico-Texan," a piece of biting satirical doggerel

written by Américo and published when he was seventeen years old.

In the late fifties, when *Pistol* was first published,
my sister Clarissa and I walked to Daddy Hargroves'
bookstore in Brownsville, and each of us bought a
copy of that fine book. Not only did I enjoy the legend part, of course, but I also admired the research
and the care taken by Américo in its presentation.

This last, I believe, is what influenced me the most
when I began my history-based Klail City series. For
this I am grateful, as I am for his unfailing kindness,
humor, and sound advice, this last, whether academic
or personal.[228]

Kay Turner is currently an independent scholar and author living in New York City. Américo Paredes was on her dissertation committee. She commented,

I've been thinking of Dr. Paredes all week. I was
in Spain at the time of his death—was in fact at the
monastery and basílica that houses the image of "una
morena milagrosa," Our Lady of Montserrat, certainly one of Guadalupe's hermanas. So even though I
didn't know Dr. Paredes was dying, I was in the right
place to wish him well on the soul's journey. Dr. Paredes was at the very center of the reason I came to folklore and to Texas to pursue it. Years later—in 1972—I
went to Mexico with a friend who had lived in Mexico
City as a child. It was an inspiring trip—my first out of
the U.S.A.—and when I came home I wanted to know
everything Mexican. This enthusiasm eventually led
to another trip for a year in Mexico and Guatemala.
In preparation, I somehow found Dr. Paredes's Mexican folktales book. It was in fact my first encounter
with the word implicating a kind of study called folklore. I carried that book with me like a bible. Read it

with a thirst that could only be slaked by finding the source of the river. Of course that river turned out to be the Río Grande and its metaphorical head in Austin was Dr. Américo Paredes.

Instructing me concerning the sacredness of motherhood, Doña Soledad "Chole" Pescina re-figured a biblical moment from her point of view: "That's why Jesus cried out [from the cross], 'Dios, Madre.' He didn't say, 'Dios, Padre.'" With a know-ing chuckle, Dr. Paredes said, "Las viejas have God on their side." And now God has Dr. Paredes on his side. The heavens gain what the earth has lost. I burn a votive candle of loving remembrance. Homenaje a Américo Paredes.[229]

The public mourning, however, was universal. On June 2, a me-morial was held at The University of Texas at Austin at the Joe E. Thompson Center. The center was filled with people who came to grieve and to celebrate their millennium man. His widow, Amelia, and his three sons, Américo, Vince, and Alan, as well as their families were in attendance. Conjunto Aztlán performed some of his favorite corridos, and Tish Hinojosa sang her corrido to the man of the cor-rido. Those in attendance reminisced and remembered the person who for much of his life had raised, carried, and defended their cultural flag with a dignity that both friends and foes could not help but respect.

Pat Jasper, founder and director of Texas Folklife Resources, said this about Américo: "I perceive someone like Dr. Paredes to have been the most public of folklorists: highly accessible, highly affirma-tive and highly subversive. He validated a community's understand-ing of itself, and he turned mainstream interpretations on their head."[230]

Richard Bauman, former colleague and professor at Indiana University, spoke about Américo's intelligence and humor: "I will remember Don Américo for many things: the generosity of his spirit, the integrity of his character, the brilliance of his mind. But I want to celebrate him today for two things that have stood out for me as I have thought of him this past couple of weeks, his humor and his voice ... some of you will remember how forgetful he was with names. On one occasion he forgot the name of one of our prominent and self-anointed colleagues in another department. I said Américo, you've known this guy for years. How could you have forgotten his name? 'I'll tell you,' he said. 'Every time I remember the name of some pendejo [jerk], I forget the words to a corrido, and it's not worth it.'"[231]

Jordanna Barton, former program coordinator for the Center for Mexican American Studies at The University of Texas at Austin, said that she was impressed by Paredes' scholarship even before she met him. When they did meet, his humor, wit, and light sarcasm were familiar to her because she had grown up in South Texas. She continued, "The knowledge of his struggles inspired me to continue and to reaffirm that we [Mexican Americans] belonged here at the University... He left us integrity. He left a standard for how to inter-act with people. It was a privilege to know him."[232]

The passing of Paredes became the subject of newspaper articles across the country. Joe Holley in the *New York Times* described him as "one of the founders of the Chicano Studies movement in the 1960s" and noted that *With His Pistol in His Hand* was recognized by Chicano activists at Berkeley and other universities "as an alternative telling of American history and sociology."[233] *Los Angeles Times* staff writer Elaine Woo wrote that his "seminal writings challenged con-ventional histories of life along the Texas-Mexico border and helped shape a positive cultural identity among Mexican Americans." He "was considered a pioneer in Mexican American studies." [234] The *Austin American-Statesman* carried an obituary of Paredes recognizing him as a "prolific scholarly writer of fiction and non fiction books and articles" who "leaves a large legacy of scholarly work as well as many 'intellectual children' (as he called them) who are now the leaders in their fields."[235]

David Montejano later wrote in *The Texas Observer*, that it was with the same dignity that Don Américo and Doña Amelia, who passed away a few months later, were laid to rest. In 1985 in an unpublished poem written to Nena, Américo expressed his feelings about being cremated after death. He wrote,

ÚLTIMA CARTA
Out of the mass of legend and romance
Given to us as holy in a book
Too often edited
One thing is certain, that we all must die.
Who then forbids us to recall the past,
Doubling the riches that our lives have given us,
And all the pain as well,
A past that makes up more than half my life
And even more of yours.

Since we cannot relive those years, unsay
All of the words we said to one another,
Utter the ones we yearned so much to speak
But never could. Or would.
Let us think of the past as but one form
Of present-time.
For we must look upon the present-past
Reflected in the mirror of our memory
And doing so we can avoid the snakes
Writhing around its head.

Then, perhaps, we can truly understand
That we have lived.

The dead past does not bury its own dead,
They tag along until the final-present.
And then when that final-present comes, I ask
You should not fear of giving me to fire,
My dearest love, my friend.

In doing so
You simply will be adding from without
To what has been inside these many years,
A burning so intense that it has scorched
Those who have touched me.
Specially you—too candid, too straightforward
To suspect the fire inside, till you
Were also burned and hardened to withstand
The demons in me.

So do not go against my last desire.
Let me burn!
Don't let me become the food of those fat worms
That call themselves morticians
Who suck your flesh and blood. And then they bury
A waxen image, nicely rouged, in what
They call a grave.
Let me burn!
Let me burn!
Till the volcano in my guts explodes
Like a Bengal light.

And then, sometimes I dream
That you perhaps will also choose the flames,
Forever lost to Chucho Christ
Because of me, your lover.
And when the Trump has made its mighty racket
And other bodies rise from slime and dust,
The two of us shall wander bodiless
Through outer space, each in our own trajectory,
And every time we meet, then I will say:
¡Vuelan, vuelan mis cantares!—
And your voice will come drifting back to me:
— ¡Hasta luegito!—[236]

Throughout much of his life, Don Américo had spent time at South Padre Island. La Isla del padre Ballí had been a place for summer visits for the Paredes family for many years and a Thanksgiving respite for family reunions during his last years. His sons and their families continue this tradition. In late October 1999, I received a phone call from Vince. He asked if I would lead the Paredes family to the mouth of the Río Grande. I agreed. On November 26, 1999, his three sons, their families, some of the Paredes relatives from Brownsville, my nephew Douglas Hinojosa, and I accompanied Don Américo and Doña Amelia on their last voyage. After meeting at Manfred del Castillo's home, we drove in a caravan of four-wheel-drive vehicles and vans to Boca Chica Beach. The street ended at the same Gulf where explorers, pirates, colonists, soldiers, tourists, and narcos had stopped before. We turned right, drove on the beach, and reached the mouth of the Río Bravo at about 11:45 a.m. There, near the collapsing sand of the river's edge, something occurred that I will never forget. Vince read "El Río Grande," the poem Américo had written over sixty years before. I read "Don Américo," a poem that I wrote shortly after his death.

Américo Paredes

Hombre derecho con las raíces en el corazon
Te recuerdo

Hombre educado y honrado de dos países y de dos
    épocas
Te aprecio

Hombre que cruzaste las líneas del tiempo
Y el río del destino
Salvando almas sin héroes
Te respeto

Cancionero que me cantaste mis canciones

Poeta que me escribiste mi dolor
Profesor que me enseñaste mi cultura
Amigo que me regalaste mi orgullo

Te celebro siempre y
Y nunca te olvidaré[237]

Américo Paredes
(English)

Righteous man whose roots are in your very heart
I remember you

Educated and honored man of two countries and
    two eras
I value you

Man who crossed the lines of time
And the river of destiny
Rescuing souls without heroes
I respect you

Balladeer who sang me my songs
Poet who wrote about my pain
Professor who taught me about my culture
Friend who gave me my pride

I will always celebrate you and
I will never forget you

At high noon on that sunny fall day, Vince and I took off our shoes, rolled up our pant legs, and walked to a juncture where the blue-green waters of the Gulf of Mexico lapped into the rushing brown waters of the Río Grande. There, Vince released some of the ashes of his father and his mother. A flowing current carried the ashes toward what was once Nuevo Santander, south of the Río Bravo. As we returned to the others waiting on the shore, a lone, viejita pescadora (old fisherwoman) wearing a migrant bonnet searched for a spot among the veteran fall fishermen. They stood next to their rod holders with cañas and carretas (rods and reels), poised for the strike from the elusive kurbina (red drum). There are moments in our lives when time does seem to stand still and there are people in our lives, whose dignity and passion for justice transcend the time of their physical presence on this earth. November 26, 1999, was one of those moments, and Don Américo Paredes was one of those people.

As the ashes of Don Américo disappeared into the Río Grande, I realized that his life had gone full circle from Brownsville to the Far East to Austin, Texas, and back to his roots in the Valley. His family and I embraced. Some of us cried because we knew that we had done what Américo and Amelia had wanted. They were at peace and for that moment so were we.

Américo was a scholar. His prolific research will no doubt be investigated for many years to come. Yet he was more than a folklorist or writer. He was an academic activist who used the power of his pen to write what had rarely been written, to document what had rarely been documented and to define what had rarely been defined.

Scholars continue to speak and write about his work, his life, and his legacy. At the 2001 Américo Paredes Symposium, professors from across the country spoke about what he wrote and what he meant to them. Those who wrote about him usually did so because in some way or another, his scholarship affected their lives. Many applauded his courage and the precedents he established; others, the sheer power of his words. Most owed a debt of gratitude to Américo Paredes. There is something to be said about an individual who champions what is just, what is right, and what is the truth, and who does it so convincingly that friends as well as enemies respect him.

As a husband, he was dedicated and caring. His wife, Amelia, loved him unconditionally until his death. As a father he was strict yet insightful. He expected from his sons what he expected from himself: the very best that they could do. His daughter, Julie, was the love of his life. As a teacher he was demanding but fair. Students were intimidated by his expectations, yet enlightened by his knowledge.

As a man he was impatient with mediocrity, almost too cognizant of his own professorial tasks, and obsessed with time. On occasions, he felt as if he were one step ahead of death, lamenting that he had not done enough in the time that he had been given. At times he was frustrated and short tempered because of it.

Since his death, two schools have been named in his honor. In January of 2000, Américo Paredes Middle School opened in Austin, and in January of 2002, Américo Paredes Elementary School opened in Brownsville. Today, students at these schools proudly honor his name with their academic excellence.

In 2005 Vince Paredes commented about his father's death and that day in November at the mouth of the Río Grande. He said, "there's really no such thing as closure but there was a certain feeling, a brief higher level of peace… The memory by the sea is symbolic of everything he was."[238]

I know Américo would be the last person to accept the label of hero because he told me so, but when I first sat face-to-face with him in his Austin home, I thought differently. I realized that he had sung and written for my mother's generation and that his literary courage had inspired my generation. As he spoke to me he did so with the fire of a young poet in his eyes. What he had done for many of us for so many years was nothing less than heroic.

Américo Paredes' professorial career was by many accounts no less than brilliant. His abilities in the classroom brought out the best in his students. His expertise as a scholar garnered him national and international accolades. Paredes not only wrote well, but defended his writing with knowledge and honor. Although he retired from full-time teaching in 1984, he continued to teach part-time and continued his research until his failing health overcame him. Américo Paredes died in 1999 and left a legacy of scholarship and teaching that led the way to serious research in an area that had long been overlooked. And although he lived in the Valley only one third of his life, the border community was important to him all of his life and for that, the academic community is a better place.

UNEDITED TRANSCRIPTION OF FAVORITE INTERVIEW WITH DR. AMÉRICO PAREDES

September 22, 1994

Dr. Américo Paredes: Okay. How do you want to lead off?

Medrano: Today is September 22, 1994. We are very pleased to be here at the home of Américo Paredes, Professor Emeritus at The University of Texas at Austin. Dr. Paredes what can you tell us about your childhood? Where were you born? About your parents? Where did you grow up?

Dr. Américo Paredes: I was born in Brownsville; I'm a Brownsville boy, on September 3, 1915, during the height of the border troubles when there was an ethnic cleansing, to use current term, along the border when Rangers and others murdered a number of Mexicans and intimidated a lot of others to leave the country; in other words, so the country could be developed. That's why we have grapefruit orchards and all of that in the Brownsville area.

Medrano: And your parents, what can you tell us about your parents?

Dr. Américo Paredes: Well, my father came from people that colonized the area in 1749. They came north with Escandon, but they had settled in the area around Nuevo León in 1580. They were part of a colony of Sephardic Jews that were brought over by Carbajal y Cueva. Now the Jews had been given a choice after 1492 either to leave the country or become Christianized. Many of them remained practicing their religion in secret. Luis Carbajal y Cueva was one of them and rose in esteem. He had come to Mexico once and participated in the defeat and capture of a power that English history doesn't talk about, John Hawkins… About the time other colonists were moving into New Mexico in 1580, and he brought more than 100 families. So these people married each other. So my father's people stayed where anti-clerics were. I said in one of my articles they didn't intermarry much, but my father did. The other matter of intermarriage broke down in the 1860s. He married someone whose parents had come down from Spain. My mother's father was from Asturias and my mother was born on the border, but her father José María Vidal was a Catalan…so that is my background, I would say.

Medrano: You were born in Brownsville. What recollections do you have of your early years growing up, going to school? What do you remember about the city, the school system, and about your own education?

Dr. Américo Paredes: Well, it was a very peaceful setting. Now it is not unfortunately, but we grew up during the Depression; by that I mean my friends Sabas Klahn, who died not too long ago, and Roberto Ramírez of another family there. We had no money so we often would go out walking anywhere. No danger, that was before the roads and smuggling, but that didn't bother us. Mostly smuggling was tequila. In other words drugs was not a problem or what are known as drug lords nowadays.

Medrano: What do you recall about the downtown area, something special about walking in el centro?

Dr. Américo Paredes: Well, it was something like a Mexican town, but we didn't have a plaza, but Elizabeth Street and Washington Street, to a certain extent, acted like Saturday evening because at that time all the farmers and ranchers came to town on Saturday, and the girls, including some from Matamoros would walk along Elizabeth Street, and on the other side the boys would walk the other way or talk to them, try to court them. That existed at that time. Washington Street was still part of downtown; and then, of course, from Washington Street on we had streets named for presidents and those Spanish speaking people, who were not really Anglos but the leaders of the towns. Anglos lived on the other side of Elizabeth Street; on that side, streets were named after saints in Spanish. But I lived really, my memory is divided a certain ways. My father had been the oldest son and they had land on what is now Texas, south of the Nueces, which then was part of the province of Nuevo Santander and Tamaulipas. They had to sell out. Though they managed to sell out to one of the big cattle barons that was married to a Mexican cattle rancher. He married Petra Vela, viuda de Vidal. The person that put pressure on him was King, who would send goons to scare his cattle and do things of that sort, and King just wanted them to pack up and leave. Kenedy brought a better price and allowed them to take their cattle and remove their horses and go south of the Río Grande. So he settled over there. Finally, he ended up there, since he didn't have any land of his own. Paredes had land north of the Río Grande. There still is a Paredes Line Road there. Don Tomás Paredes, who was a thinker, the brother of my great-grandfather. They settled with the Cisneros and my father, who was the oldest, was supposed to inherit the home place because he didn't have problems. So they always divided the land but the oldest would take the home place, but he was a rebel. In fact, he was mixed up in a couple of revolutions mentioned in *With His Pistol in His Hand*. He was one of those that helped Porfirio Díaz, but my father went against him... Finally he did settle there and my youngest brother Eliseo, who finally went back to Mexico, was born here and my sister... I don't think my mother was born over on the American side. But then my father decided he just didn't want to be a rancher; he wanted to be in town so he came over to Brownsville. At that time, as I understood, in 1920. Local law said all residents could vote; that was a nice twist because a lot of Mexicans were residents and were not American citizens. My father never became an American citizen. But in that period he was kind of like a political boss among Mexicans. I use some of that in *George Washington Gómez*. But his second brother, Vicente, I named one of my sons after him, took over the rancho and my younger brother and I would go every summer until I was fourteen. We would go over there and the rest of the family would go to San Antonio where my mother had a brother or to the beach or so on. We would head immediately across the river the back way. Everyone had little boats hidden on the edges, and we would stay there three months living like Mexicans, listening to people tell their stories. My father would come down sometimes also, and then at the end of August, they would drive us back to Brownsville and once there I was living in another world, because I learned English at home and didn't have a language problem.

Medrano: What was it like being a Chicano in a public school?

Dr. Américo Paredes: I think that probably around that time we had one grammar school. I think remnants of it are now Annie Putegnat School. It was a two-story building. It had an iron fence which had been destroyed by that time. In the lower grades ninety percent were Mexicans, so really the Anglos were a minority. Sometimes, if they did not watch out they might be beaten up and everybody spoke Spanish. They were not supposed to because of English language rule. I'm sure you are aware. It began around World War II [*sic*] and was aimed at the Germans, not the Mexicans. But after the war the Germans continued speaking German. I remember in Fredericksburg, I had my car repaired there and two young mechanics were doing what we used to do in the Valley. I guess you still do it. They would be speaking in German and English, and one would say something in English and the other would answer in German, but they saddled us with that until fairly recently, but not in my time. My first grade teacher was Ms. Josefina Castañeda, sister of Dr. Carlos Castañeda, who grew up in, he was born across the river. I don't know if he was born in Mier or one of the little places, but he grew up in Brownsville. He went to Saint Joseph's with my brother. So I had no problems with that, but the other kids... I remember by the time I went to school the Civil War in Mexico had been going on for sometime and people were coming, fleeing, and we would get a number of those in school. Now they had problems because they couldn't speak English and because some of the Tejano kids would pick on them and that is when I heard the word *mojado* first. It does not mean wetbacks for God's sake. I remember them chasing one little boy yelling "*mojado, mojado*" and knocked him down and they felt behind his ear. That is where they were supposed to be *mojados* after crossing the river. It was only when the Anglos finally began to think of these people. They could not call them the wets because of the prohibition of wets vs. dries, so they were the ones that called them *los mojados*. It happened that about the time that the word wetback became very well known, I first heard of J. Frank Dobie. In 1936 I began to work at *The Herald*. I had seen the man once. Now this was in high school or junior college. We were together. We were at the same auditorium. He came and spoke to us. That parody of *George Washington Gómez* is based on that, though I didn't feel anything.

Medrano: You attended junior college? Do you have any memories of that or any recollections of educational experiences there?

Dr. Américo Paredes: Yes, things began to change. Really what began to change was the Depression. I was doing very well in school, but the Depression wiped us out. My eldest brother and my father had a dry goods store on Washington Street. It was cattycorner from Manatou. I don't know whether Manatou exists now. It was called La Campana. My second brother had a very good job at Brownsville Title Company. In fact, he was looking for all those titles and discovering a lot of the chanchuyas. It just happened that my brother Eliseo was a gambler. He kept the better the business [*sic*] the more he put into it, and in 1929 things were doing so well that he even borrowed money to put more into the store. The crash finished it. Besides at the bank where he had the money, the cashier had being gambling on his own on the stock market and he had been using the money. He later went to prison, so he was wiped out. My brother went to see Dr. del Castillo because he had a bad allergy, and the doctor told him that he was tubercular and he better leave his job. So he had just married. His wife was a Garza; in fact, she was an aunt of the city manager here in Austin, Jesus Garza. So he, but her father had a big dairy farm, so he went and worked over there to be out in the fresh air, of course, getting up at three o'clock in the morning and working all day. Finally, it turns out that he wasn't tubercular, so he went back and he got a job, but during that period our family was wiped out. I started having to work a little bit; my grades went down to a certain extent and I started running into trouble with high school teachers.

By the time I got to high school and even to junior high, the situation had been reversed because all those Mexicanos that had been with me in grammar school had dropped out, and there were relatively few. For example in one class, I remember, I was never able to find out why the lady that taught that class, Ms. Bell was her name, married a man that came and visited me here. But in one class, four of us were put into a special Ancient History class. The other three were Anglos, except for me. It was a real wonderful thing but through junior high my friends started dropping out. Really, the friends I had in college had gone to Saint Joseph's. And there I had problems, especially with some very stupid teachers. I think the reason was that, and this might come up on the most important things as far as education for our people. Three things: money, money, money. I mean I'm sure some of those teachers came from other places. They must not have been able to get a job somewhere else. They could only get a job there in Brownsville. I had especially trouble with a teacher I had in Junior English. For my term project I wrote a short story that was published in the annual when I was just a junior in high school and this was in the junior college annual. I made A's in everything else but she failed me because I would not tell her that I liked Walt Whitman. I did not like Walt Whitman because all the poetry I had heard was with rhyme and rhythm both in Spanish and English. She gives me a book of Walt Whitman and tells me this is great poetry. I said this is gibberish. This is prose; I don't understand it. And we had several fights in there and she felt I had insulted her and when I came back I went to take junior English again, the principal told me just to go apologize to her. Well, I apologized to her. Not until I came here that I found out she gave me a C anyway in that class. But there we had a prejudice but not straight out because some teachers, Anglos, also were very decent. Very decent. Some were not.

The thing is that when I was finishing my junior year there was a contest given by Trinity College which was in Waxahachie, not here in San Antonio [*sic*], a poetry contest. Well, it was this junior English teacher that got it, I suppose. She just put it on the bulletin board. It wasn't announced anywhere. I wouldn't ask the lady for it. I went and got the address and sent the poem on my own. It was "A Sonnet Tonight," a very forgettable poem, but it won first prize. I found out when I was a senior already, so the principal was an Anglo. I have a higher education because of him. He was the principal of the high school and dean of the junior college. He came to see me because he had asked who sponsored this kid? And nobody knew. I told him, well, nobody did. And he said "you mean you did this all on your own?" I said yes, so he became interested in me. Now during junior college I had him. He was, had been the coach, the football coach. He had been fired as coach because when we got to high school, we had the Screaming Eagles who went all the way to the semifinals and they were defeated, so they fired him as the coach. But he became Dean of the College, and he was a good dean. I heard of the term New Deal before I ever heard of Franklin D. Roosevelt from him first. I took a course, I think it was called Civics at that time. And when we graduated my grades were so-so; he recognized me because not only had I won this prize but because of initiative of doing it on my own. Now, by the way, this is a little story... this teacher who used to be my junior English teacher... who had given me a C asked me, "what about the prize?" Well, they had given me a book cover made of tooled leather from Spain. And she said, "well it's better than having been given a book of lousy poetry." So that told me what she thought of poetry and here she was teaching poetry at the junior level.

Well, school ends and I get my high school diploma. That was it; nowhere to go, so I was standing on a street corner in Brownsville. I think it was Levee instead of Elizabeth with a few other kids. Not looking for trouble, but just standing around waiting for it to come around, I guess. But the dean and principal drove by in his little Chevy. It was a roadster with a rumble seat. And he saw me; he stopped and backed up. This was already late June, I think and he called and I went up and he said, "are you going to Junior College?" I said no. I'm not. I don't have the money for it, and he said, "did you apply for student assistantship?" I told him, what is that? Now talk about prejudice. The lady that was dean of the college was involved in this but she never thought of Mexicans as in that category. So I told him I didn't. So he said, "you write me a letter. Though the deadline was in April, you write me a letter and I'll get you an assistantship." And that is how I got to go to junior college. There were very few of us Mexicanos. I think there were three of us men that we, for the rest of the time, we were together. They used to call us El Flaco, El Chaparro, y El Grandote. And guess who was the Flaco? El Chaparro was Roberto Ramírez, who was really short. And El Grandote was Sabas Klahn, who was almost six feet. At that time being six feet was very very tall. And we made it through. But after that there was nothing. My English teacher in junior college was a very good teacher and she was a very good reader. By the way, I learned... I went to the public library and got a copy of *Leaves of Grass* and sat there reciting to myself. All of a sudden, I saw the rhythm all by myself, so I learned what Whitman was about because that woman never attempted to read to us. Now Ms. Hyman in junior college did, and she had a beautiful speaking voice. When we were ready to graduate I saw her and she said, "Mr. Paredes what do you intend to do after college?" And I told her, well I would like very much was to go to The University of Texas and get a Ph.D. in English. And at that time I was angry, but later I saw the truth of it. She said, "Mr. Paredes you have a facility with language. Why don't you try to get a job with the local paper?" And that really hurt me now but now in hindsight I see that she was right. There were no scholarships for Mexicans in 1950.

Medrano: And there were almost no Mexicans.

Dr. Américo Paredes: I came in on a U.S. Army fellowship, scholarship; you know the GI Bill. And she knew I had already written several little pieces with *The Brownsville Herald*, so I went and drove a bread truck for a while and did a few other things. Finally, I saw the light and went and got a job at *The Brownsville Herald*. But if it hadn't been for this dean. I never remember his first name. He was known as Red Irvine. He was fired, by the way, while I was a sophomore. O. B. García was a lawyer in Brownsville. Once he told me that he became a book agent, but I never heard from him again. But I think if I had not had those two years of junior college, courtesy of Red Irvine, I would not have had the guts, if I say, to come back at the age of thirty-five and to start as an undergraduate here at The University of Texas. I stayed overseas in 1950, but I took a few courses by correspondence; so in twelve months straight I got my B.A. And after that, ... I asked for a job as a grader but my creative writing teacher, I went to see him and I told him would he recommend me as grader, and he looked at me and said "no, no." I thought I had really good grades... "I want to recommend you as what they call these days a teaching fellow." A teaching fellow was a teacher; you taught one course. I started teaching in 1951. And of course, I worked like hell. Let my wife run the house and everything while I worked to get two degrees and in, let's see, '51, in five years.

Medrano: What motivated you, Dr. Paredes, during those times you were here?

Dr. Américo Paredes: Well, the fact that this had been my ambition and I knew that time was running out. I mean you don't, now there are people that are coming back to school. At thirty-five you're middle-aged. I was sitting in that first year, I was sitting with young kids, but after that I went into graduate school, of course, and it was different. I wanted to get it and I wanted to give our side. I had written this novel; nobody even wanted to read it. I even forgot about it. But I had written some short stories. By the way I have a book of short stories that's out now. Nobody wanted it then. One that I wrote in 1939, "The Hammon and the Beans," I sent it all over... When I came back in 1950, again I sent it. Then, Ronnie Dugger of *The Observer*, I had been giving him some things nonfiction. And once he asked me "do you have anything for the paper, for *The Observer?*" I told him no, but I have a short story. "Well, let me see it." And he published that short story in 1963. Then Edward Simmen reprinted it in a little book called *The Chicano: From Caricature to Self-Portrait.* And it took off. I don't remember how many times it's been reprinted since then. But the situation has changed. We are no longer pariahs. They're beginning to understand, finally .What they were trying to say, I remember there is a character named Chonita in "The Hammon and the Beans." I remember one university press said they said they had liked the story, but they felt they wanted more about Chonita. They wanted the story to be cute, you know. If you were writing, you wrote about lovely señoritas.

Back to something you asked me. "Why did I work so hard to get an education?" Well, when I finished high school, the prospect I had then was working at a shoe store or a dry goods store selling shoes. And I hated that, and it certainly did not lead anywhere. I got the chance to go two years of college and, of course, that whetted my appetite. I knew that most of my other schoolmates went on to get a degree. The best I could do was get a job at *The Brownsville Herald* making $11.40 a week. And even though at the time that was more than it is today, it wasn't very much. In 1940 ... the war got started in Europe. Pan American Airways started arming planes for Great Britain. I got a job there at fifteen dollars a week. But I would still, at that time, *The Brownsville Herald, The Monitor of McAllen,* and *The Morning Star* were bought all by a man named Hubert Hudson. And all became... they continued to publish separately, but the Sunday paper was done in Brownsville and was for all of them. I still had a job there Saturdays and Sundays. I wrote a great deal for *The Brownsville Herald.* In fact, of all the articles I wrote on Mexican culture, they were used in the early Charro Days. They were cannibalized and printed and reprinted later... My salary rose to about fifteen dollars. I was getting fifteen dollars over there. At that time I got a job singing my own songs on the radio and I was paid the magnificent sum of, I love to mention that, one dollar a minute for fifteen minutes a week. So I was really making, what people like me would make at that time, a lot of money, forty-five dollars a week. Though inflation was on, I still felt that I was at a dead-end. So this is something that some people thought I was crazy to do because the job I had at Pan American was like a war job; therefore, I was exempt from the draft. Well, there were a number of reasons including the fact that some of my friends, Matías Serrata, who had played the guitar with me, was killed in France. Este muchacho, se me olvida el nombre, Morán. Miguel Morán died after action in Attu. I began to get a guilt feeling, but also I wanted to get out of Brownsville because it was a dead-end as far as education was concerned. So I just quit the job with Pan American.

And I could not volunteer because at that time this was in '44 already; they didn't want people in the Navy; they didn't want people in the Air Force. They wanted people with rifles; they weren't called grunts at the time but that is what they wanted. So they told me "go home, we'll call you." And I worked for *The Herald* for a time and they took me. And in a way it was very good for me because some-body who had been reading too many detective books saw that I was a newspaper reporter and they put me in the CID, the Criminal In-vestigation Division. Now they were supposed to be detectives. There was one other reporter from California. All the rest were former highway patrolmen, detectives, and we were supposed to be trained in law enforcement. Of course, I washed out in that and so they sent me to Seattle, and at the time the war ended anyway. So by the time I ended up in Japan in Nagoya, the war was over. Again, a lucky break. They were starting a newspaper in the base, the replacement cen-ter... There were several people there, two men: one from New York and one from San Francisco; both of them of Jewish extraction; both of them left-wing radicals, hasta las cachas, I mean one of them was a member of the Communist Party. But they were looking over and saw my name and they had read a book by Hart Stilwell, who had been my editor who had read my book [in manuscript]. He had not been offended by what I said in the novel about the Rangers, though his father was a Texas Ranger. But he was enraged about what I had said about Dobie. We fell out from that, you know. So we had a falling out on that. He was never interested in that. He published a book called *Border City* in which he was a radical reporter, very much like me in it. And these people went to see whom they could pick to work on the paper. And they asked me where I was from; I said from Brownsville. And they said, "have you heard of a book named *Border City*?" I said, well, I'm in it, I told him. So they hired me for the newspaper. And the group, they were all people with a college education. The man that became a very close friend of mine until he died recently in Germany, Horst de la Croix. He already had a Masters; the others had a least a Bachelors. So I was going in a group that really helped me orient myself there. And I stayed after. They only kept me there for another year; in 1946 I was discharged but got a job over there with the International Branch of American Red Cross, not the International Red Cross, but the American Red Cross. They had an International Branch that worked with Red Cross societies, especially Japanese, Korean, and Chinese. So I spent a year in China going around as PRO [Public Relations Officer] for China, and then I was in Korea and that really broadened my horizons. When the Red Cross, to use a current word, downsized, I no longer had a job. I got a job editing a little magazine for the Armed Forces for two years. During that time I read a lot. The section in which this magazine was also part of the college, the Armed Forces College. So I took classes in the Armed Forces College because I realized I didn't want to go back to Brownsville with just a junior college education. There wasn't anything for me to do that I would want to do. So I took a gamble and I came to UT and got the Bachelors and found that well, of course, I was much better read than most of my fellow students. After all I was thirty-five years old. I was older than most graduate students at that time, so I did very well. I did very well. And I had gotten what I wanted all this time, an education. Because it's very very necessary if you're going to, really, let's put it in the crassest terms, to have a good income.

Medrano: The word heritage is synonymous with you, Dr. Paredes, as a folklorist, activist, and as a scholar. Why is one's heritage so important?

Dr. Américo Paredes: Well, that comes back to my early days when I used to listen to the old men talk. And then I would spend three months over there and I would come and take history which told us a completely different view. I remember arguing with my teacher about the Monroe Doctrine. Some of the things I got in there because she felt it was something very good for Latin America. I told her no. I have it verbatim in this novel. She said, "what if you have a situation with a little boy with candy and then a big boy comes and tries to take the candy from him; then another big boy comes and pushes the big boy away." I said yes, but then the other big boy takes the candy away from the little boy. Of course, she allowed those things. So I was very much aware, I was certainly not the only one, that what we were taught in school at that time and what we knew in our hearts and what our elders told us was different. That our heritage was not being, not being given the respect that it deserved so what I did in *The Herald* during Charro Days was milder, you know. Showing them; this song, for example most Anglos I knew thought that "Sobre las olas" was a German waltz, which was "Over the Waves." So I wrote an article about Juventino Rosas and how he had written it and a number of other songs. So those things, but more important to me, was to show what had been done, the injustices that had been done to our people and the value to our heritage. Much of that fell on deaf ears until I finally was able to come here. First, I had almost forgotten the novel. What I did *With His Pistol in His Hand* was do the same job from a nonfiction view point and using Gregorio Cortez as a major figure in it. But I was not the only one. There were people working on that, even, the LULAC at the time. They were very timid, very assimilationist, yet they would come out once in a while. One of my younger brothers, Eleazar, he's dead now, he took a course and that was later. I never had that happen to me where he was told Mexicans, rather a textbook said Mexicans lived under trees, and he had a big fight with the teacher and he was expelled from school. So one of my older brothers went to see the LULAC people, and they straightened the matter out. So that was happening all along.

The thing was that most of what our people knew was in corridos and in legends and oral history. And I wanted to bring those things to the majority because I felt there were enough people of good will among the Anglos, which if they saw our side, they would really react. And in a talk I gave at Sacramento State after George Sánchez died; there was an activist. I made that point because Edward Simmen, who did do a great deal, he was one of those that awakened, did say in his book, *The Chicanos: From Caricature to Self-Portrait.* He said, "the lazy bandido sleeping against the adobe wall finally has awakened." And I challenged him on that, saying we have been awake. People have been writing in Spanish mostly; that was our problem. So few of our elders knew English. They'd been writing. Another one was Perales, Alonso Perales, *En defensa de mi raza.* And they had been organizing and very often being put down, sometimes violently because of that. And what I said there was that the people who had awakened to a new era were the Anglos. Because it was about that time that Anglos of good will began to see our side, and we needed their help to be able to make ourselves heard. That's why this story "The Hammon and the Beans" got published by an Anglo of good will, Ronnie Dugger, after a lot of Anglos refused to see that there was anything in it. So we were lucky in a sense; I was. The English Department has always been liberal at Texas and they were willing to listen to me, even to allow me to get a Ph.D. in English, which was written about a ballad in Spanish about a historical figure. Chicanos very often don't know where to place me, whether to say I'm a historian, or I'm an anthropologist or a literary figure. *With His Pistol in His Hand* had all those things. I don't think I could have done that at that time in the fifties in any other department; perhaps in Anthropology because Anthropology has always been... I didn't even know that the Anthropology Department existed at that time.

Medrano: What kind of comments can you make to children about their abuelitos and abuelitas? Why is it so important for children to still communicate with them? Sometimes in modern times, with so much technology, we forget where part of our history is and part of our history is in our family. Why is it so important to communicate?

Dr. Américo Paredes: One of my dreams, I have never fulfilled it though some people were working on it. Tony—and do you know Joe Graham? Well, he got his Ph.D. with me also. Some thing that I call Operation Castaña. Do you know what a castaña is among our people? It's a trunk. That's where our people put documents, things they had written, books they had read; all of those things went into the castaña. And I wanted my students to go and talk to their abuelitos and abuelitas to see about what they had and to give them to their teachers who were interested in this sort of thing. And that has been done to some extent. Not only does it further their knowledge of people but it gives the students self-esteem. To know that just because their grandparents don't know much English or any English at all, that they're dumb. They were probably writing decimas or other kinds of poetry, and nobody knows about it. So that I think, going back to one's roots, is very important.

Medrano: You founded the Mexican American Studies Department here. How did you feel when you were the first one ever to create such a department?

Dr. Américo Paredes: Well, there we had a lot of problems. They tried. We had a dean here who was supposed to be a liberal; the only liberal thing about him was that he hated Frank Erwin who was a member of the Board of Regents. His name was Silber... He was racist as he could be, but most of the Anglo people thought he was a liberal. After all, he was locking horns with Frank Erwin and Frank Erwin was no raging liberal himself, obviously. But he tried to hamstring this thing by pitting the Blacks against us. He took charge because he scared the administration by telling them that if we didn't have an Ethnic Studies Program immediately there would be burnings in the streets and so on. So he took charge and he established a program of Ethnic Studies, not Mexican American Studies, not Black Studies. And he got a retired, old retired professor, a Black professor to run it. Of course, he thought he had been given the job of setting up Black Studies. So I had to clash with him. For example, he wanted the program to have Swahili. All students had to learn Swahili, but Swahili was never an African language. It was a lingua franca that the Arabs developed while they were doing slaving expeditions in East Africa. But he opposed my wanting to have Spanish. And you know the old saying, "the one thing an acting director cannot do is act." So we just sat there and the whole thing was withering on the vine. Finally, that's a long long story with a number of . . . we could talk about for several hours. We finally, I convinced the new dean, Robert King, who was hated or was hated by a number of students, but to us he was good. I finally convinced him to let me find what people we had on campus that were ready to take over because I insisted that the director would have to have tenure so they would go and bang on the dean's desk and not be fired, not be terminated. So I was allowed to look around with a committee, and we chose two people, Ricardo Romo and Rodolfo de la Garza. The dean chose Rodolfo de la Garza. He was very good. Ricardo Romo went to San Antonio and did very well over there. Now, we have him here. So really it was with Rudy de la Garza that we really got going with a good budget and somebody capable and not be afraid to talk back to the administration.

Medrano: Dr. Paredes what do you consider your greatest successes and your greatest disappointments?

Dr. Américo Paredes: Well, I don't know. They're all so mixed up together you know that I would not use the words my greatest successes because anything I did, there were a lot of people working with me. But I think I never would have founded before I founded Mexican American Studies Center. I founded the Folkloric Center and we became the Anthropology Department. Here is one of the few departments that has five, what do we call them, five concentrations. Usually, you have Social Cultural Anthropology, Social Linguistics,

Physical Anthropology, and Archeology. Here after I had been there, we had a fifth one, Folklore. And from there I went to the Mexican American Studies Program. The Mexican American Studies Program has been doing very well. I cannot claim credit for it. All I can say, the way I can say about folklore was that I planted the seeds and saw the seedlings grow about this tall, but then others really saw them become a forest. But I am very happy about that. I'm very happy, for example, to go to campus now when I can and have coffee with a growing number of Mexicanos that we have in different departments. Not only in the humanities, but we have Armendariz, for example, in mathematics.

Medrano: Could you say a few words to the parents who will be listening to you speak about the importance of keeping their children in school?

Dr. Américo Paredes: It is very important and most important of all from the parents' viewpoint is helping their children, giving them support as much as possible. Of course, that is not feasible for some parents whose English is limited but perhaps to find someone to tutor the students but make them feel well. As the Chicanos have said, "Que si se puede; si se puede hacer." What we need, of course, is money because parents have to pull a child out of school to help support the family, what can you do? But very often, perhaps one of the things that might be done is to have volunteers, bilingual volunteers who are willing to help the family. I have been reading a, I read a manuscript done by Harriet Romo; she is the wife of Ricardo Romo. She's an Anglo, by the way, but her Spanish is extremely good. She was in Latin America with these groups that went over there. And she is in sociology, and she and another, I think someone in social ed., have a book. It's been accepted by the UT Press on, it was a study of dropouts in Austin where the situation is much better. And she gives us one example from her own personal experience; it was a mother that knew no English and they were stonewalling her. So she, Mrs. Romo herself, decided to act for the mother. And she got stonewalled. She would make an appointment with an assistant principal.

She would show up and the assistant principal wasn't there and very much of that happened. And I'm sure if it can happen in Austin, it could happen in our public schools, too. So perhaps a group of young people perhaps with college education that could help, especially the parents that can not do it for themselves, that would be a very very important thing. Because we need it, and the fact the situation down there sadly is not the situation that I saw when I was young. You have real problems but things are happening. So, I hope my alma mater down there is part of my Austin alma mater, so I could say that all my degrees are from UT.

Medrano: Do you have a favorite corrido, something that really stands out in your mind that you've had for a long time?

Dr. Américo Paredes: Well, of course my favorite corrido from an intellectual viewpoint is el corrido de Gregorio Cortez or as I like to kid, I like it because I got a Ph.D. out of it. But that is probably, you have life completely reproducing oral tradition. Because what oral tradition says in the corrido, here was a peaceful man who was goaded, either one of his relatives is killed and then he rises in wrath, kills several sheriffs, and either is captured and killed or gets to the other side. And Gregorio Cortez, from what everybody has said, and this includes the warden of the prison he was in, the sheriffs who had captured him, all said he was a cool man, very intelligent. That's why I hate this garbage that was put out as a movie. They showed the man actually bawling out loud. Everybody says he was completely, in fact, he would speak in Spanish and the translator would translate, and he would tell him in Spanish "te equivocaste." He knew enough English but he made friends with the people that captured him. So I thought he was the ideal person to present my case.

Musically, el corrido de Jacinto Treviño, which is completely ahistorical, is a favorite and is a favorite among Chicanos. It's ahistorical because it's an amalgam of two historical corridos, one about Jacinto Treviño and another about Ignacio Treviño. Now, I have el corrido, the original of Ignacio Treviño in my book, *The Texas Mexican Cancionero.* By the time I published that, I had not been able to find anybody who knew the original Jacinto Treviño. Somebody who published... you know these are ephemeral, little papers that appear, appeared. This is in the 1970s. He wrote me and told me he had found the corrido and he published it. I wrote him to ask him permission for me to use it to write an article. It's still in my file... I mean you just have one life and you can't do everything at the same time. But Ignacio Treviño fought against the Rangers in a saloon in Brownsville, Texas. He was a policeman at the time the Mexicanos controlled Brownsville. And the Rangers and the sheriff's deputies who belonged to another party came and killed one Ranger who was detailed to assassinate José Crixell. Crixell, by the way, is not an English name; it's either Catalan or Gallego. They still use the "x" to stand for the "sh" sound. José Crixell, Mexicano, he was sheriff, no the marshal, the city marshal, and the Ranger called Mac something, I can't remember his name right now, killed him down in the Market Square by using two pistols. He knew that Crixell would come around, do his rounds, and he would come to the market square, tether his horse and then go have coffee. So first this Ranger, MacAlister was his name. This Ranger resigned from the Ranger force. The Rangers were in a camp outside. He came into town; he sat where he knew Crixell would come. On a chair straddling it with his hands and arms on the chair, with his pistol very visible here and his hat on his lap. But in his lap he had another pistol. So he had told him, "Hey Joe, come here." And Crixell started walking to him... when he got close he murdered him. Then the Rangers and deputies came in and started shooting up the place. Todos los Mexicanos, como algunos por ejemplo, yo conocí a ese viejito, se llamaba Warvisky Polaco pero era Mexicano. Murió en Matamoros y casi todos se escaparon para Matamoros.

A Ignacio Treviño lo encorralaron en la cantina de Elefante Blanco que era de otro Crixell. They shot each other; fired at each other. About the only casualties were a couple of kegs of beer and a lot of bottles. So finally somebody arranged a truce and Ignacio Treviño was able to leave for Matamoros. That's why el corrido says "en la cantina ve que se agarraron a balazos; por donde quiera salta-ban botellas hechas pedazos." But Jacinto Treviño was in el Ranchi-to, working for an Anglo, he and his brother. And the Anglo was, the brother was working on a tractor and the rancher wasn't happy with the work he had done, so he called him a son of … and he said he started coming down. By the time he got down the rancher had a big heavy wrench and he hit him on his head and killed him. So Jacinto's brother heard about that and he came but he had a pistol and he killed the rancher and crossed over to Matamoros. So then a cousin of Jacinto was hired by the Rangers and deputies to lure Jacinto across and he agreed to come. But not being exactly stupid he came a couple of hours before the tryst and he was hiding already when two cars with rinches and deputies arrived. And they got off and, and of course, the first one, he had a rifle, the first one he killed was his cousin and then he killed, I think, two or three of the lawmen and wounded several others. And apparently, they started shooting at each other because there were two cars. And he escaped to Mata-moros and he lived there. In those days they still had cocheros, you know, coaches. And he was a very peaceful man. In fact I understand that somebody, you know you see that the old wild western movies, the young gunslinger challenges the other gunslinger. He wanted to fight Jacinto Treviño, and he wouldn't fight him. But that was Jacinto Treviño. And by the way the story is that Treviño didn't kill anybody, that he was, that they had shot each other; after all Mexicans can't shoot. Well, I hope you can get something.

Medrano: This is great! Well, thank you!

Graduate Studies Syllabus
Center for Intercultural Studies in Folklore and Ethnomusicology
University of Texas at Austin

Provided to the author by Frances Terry. Not so much a syllabus as a table of contents for a coursepack, which the students were expected to read in its entirety. Note how many pages they had to master!

GRADUATE SYLLABUS FOR FOLKLORE

Contents
Introduction

Introduction

By virtue of its comprehensiveness and annotations, this bibliography is designed to meet the needs of (1) Folklore majors, and (2) Anthropology students for whom Folklore is one of two areas of concentration.

Note:

1. Items marked with an asterisk (*) are essential; professional competence in Folklore demands thorough familiarity with these works.

2. Items marked with a dash (-) are important works which should be known, but not necessarily in detail. In certain cases these works are "classics" in the field and of great historical importance, but need to be read with an especially critical eye in the light of contemporary folkloristic thought.

3. In cases where an entire collection of essays (reader, symposium, etc.) has been listed, the individual articles have not been given separate entries; special care should be taken in examining publications of this kind to avoid missing important essays.

4. Students should develop competence in each section of the syllabus; this calls for familiarity with reference tools and command of the literature on theory and method, genres, and related subjects.

5. While the syllabus has not been organized in terms of specific cultural or geographic areas, there is ample material for the development of real concentrations in addition to the concentrations in note 4, and students will be required to become proficient in the folklore

and folkloristics of selected culture areas of their own choice.
6. Every effort will be made to keep the syllabus up to date; be sure
to check with your local folklorist before taking your exams.

ENDNOTES

Note to Introduction

1. Margot Torres, Tribute to Dr. Américo Paredes, November 24, 1998, University of Texas at Brownsville-Texas Southmost College.

Notes to Chapter 1

2. Arnoldo De Leon, *Mexican American in Texas: A Brief History* (Arlington Heights, IL: Harlan Davidson Pub., 1993), 37-42.
3. Américo Paredes, Interview with author, September 22, 1994, Austin, Texas. Reprinted as Appendix 1 in this book.
4. David Montejano, *Anglos and Mexicans in the Making of Texas, 1836–1986* (Austin: University of Texas Press, 1987), 117.
5. Paredes interview, September 22, 1994.
6. James A. Irby, *Backdoor at Bagdad*, Monograph 53 (El Paso: The University of Texas at El Paso, Texas Western Press, 1979), 6–7.
7. Alan Paredes interview with author, December 9, 2001, Austin, Texas.
8. Paredes interview, September 22, 1994.
9. Paredes interview, September 22, 1994.
10. Paredes interview, September 22, 1994.
11. Paredes interview, September 22, 1994.
12. Paredes interview, September 22, 1994.
13. Américo Paredes, Interview with author, March 25, 1995, Austin, Texas.
14. Paredes interview, September 22, 1994.
15. Paredes interview, September 22, 1994.
16. Paredes interview, September 22, 1994.
17. Paredes interview March 25, 1995.

18. Paredes interview March 25, 1995.
19. Blanca Paredes, Interview with author, October 7, 2003, Brownsville, Texas.
20. Manfred del Castillo, Interview with author, March 22, 2000, Brownsville, Texas.
21. Paredes interview, September 22, 1994.
22. Manfred del Castillo interview, March 22, 2000.

Notes to Chapter 2

23. William Buford Beeson, Interview with author, July 23, 2003, Brownsville, Texas.
24. Paredes interview, September 22, 1994.
25. Paredes interview, September 22, 1994.
26. Américo Paredes, "The Tide," *The Palmegian Yearbook*, 1933, p. 20.
27. Manfred del Castillo interview, March 22, 2000.
28. Paredes interview, September 22, 1994.
29. Paredes interview, September 22, 1994.
30. Américo Paredes, "The Taste of the Habanero," p. 1, 1935, unpublished freshman English essay, Américo Paredes Papers, Benson Latin American Collection, General Libraries University of Texas at Austin. Hereafter cited as Paredes Papers.
31. Américo Paredes, "The Evening," p. 1, 1935, unpublished freshman English essay, Paredes Papers.
32. Américo Paredes, "Afternoon in a Cantina," p. 1, 1935, unpublished freshman English essay, Paredes Papers.
33. Paredes interview, March 25, 1995.
34. Paredes interview, March 25, 1995.
35. Paredes interview, September 22, 1994.
36. Américo Paredes, "Black Roses," 1936, unpublished manuscript preface, Paredes Papers.
37. Américo Paredes, "Black Roses."
38. Américo Paredes, "Black Roses."
39. Américo Paredes, "Black Roses."
40. Emilio Zamora, "The Américo Paredes Papers," *The Journal of South Texas* 15 (Fall 2002): 16.
41. Américo Paredes, *Cantos de Adolescencia* (Houston: Arte Publico Press, 2007), 7.

42. Paredes, *Cantos de Adolescencia*, 9.

43. Paredes interview March 25, 1995.

44. Paredes, *Cantos de Adolescencia*, 7.

45. Paredes, *Cantos de Adolescencia*, 7.

46. Américo Paredes, *Between Two Worlds* (Houston: Arte Público Press, 1991), 15–16.

47. This poem was reprinted in *Between Two Worlds*, 26.

48. Paredes interview, September 22, 1994.

49. Narciso Martínez , Interview with author, November 12, 1991, La Paloma, Texas.

50. Paredes interview March 25, 1995.

51. Américo Paredes, *Between Two Worlds*, 42–43.

52. Paredes interview, September 22, 1994.

53. Paredes interview March 25, 1995.

54. Richard Bauman, Introduction, *Folklore and Culture on the Texas-Mexican Border*, by Américo Paredes (Austin: The University of Texas at Austin Center for Mexican American Studies, 1993), xv.

55. Américo Paredes, "Old Notes."

56. James Patterson, *America in the Twentieth Century* (San Diego: Harcourt Brace Jovanovich Publishers, 1989), 179–81.

57. Paredes interview March 25, 1995.

58. Paredes interview March 25, 1995.

59. Américo Paredes, "Crystal City Baccalaureate Talk," 1972, Paredes Papers.

60. Angélica Silva, Interview with Cristina Ballí and Manuel F. Medrano, September 13, 2003, Brownsville, Texas.

61. Emilio Zamora, "The Américo Paredes Papers," 2.

62. Antonia Medrano, Interview with author, November 21, 1991, Brownsville, Texas.

63. "Chelo Silva," North of the Border Radio Program, KMBH, September 6, 2003, Harlingen, Texas.

64. Angélica Silva interview, September 13, 2003.

65. Teresa Palomo Acosta, Interview with Cristina Ballí, September 5, 2003, Austin, Texas.

66. Américo Paredes, Far East Notebook, p. 117, Series 1, Box 12, 1947–1948, Paredes Papers.

Notes to Chapter 3

67. Paredes interview March 25, 1995.
68. A Guide to the Hart Stilwell Papers, Southwest Writers Collection, Texas State University. http://www.lib.utexas.edu/taro/tsusm/00069/tsu-00069.html Accessed June 24, 2008.
69. Paredes interview March 25, 1995.
70. Paredes interview March 25, 1995.
71. Américo Paredes, "Chaplain Dalton Won't Get Cold Feet," *The G Eye Opener*, December 1945. Copy found in Paredes Papers.
72. Américo Paredes, "Half Million Japanese Parade in Tokyo Streets in May Day Celebration," *Pacific Stars and Stripes*, May 2, 1946. Copy found in Paredes Papers.
73. Américo Paredes, *Between Two Worlds*, 108.
74. Presentation by José Limón, Américo Paredes Symposium, May 3, 2001, Austin, Texas.
75. Américo Paredes, first page of letter from Shanghai, March 15, 1947, Américo Paredes Papers.
76. Américo Paredes, Far East Notebook, p. 106, Series 1, Box 12, 1947–1948, Paredes Papers.
77. Post-interview conversation with Américo Paredes and Amelia Nagamine, September 22, 1994.
78. Américo Paredes, "Inventory," p. 4, Paredes Papers.
79. Américo Paredes, Letter to Amelia Paredes, April 6, 1948, Paredes Papers.

Notes to Chapter 4

80. Paredes interview, September 22, 1994.
81. Américo Paredes, Far East Notebook, p. 111, Series 1, Box 12, 1947–1948, Paredes Papers.
82. Lorenzo Paredes, Interview with author, March 15, 2000, Brownsville, Texas.
83. Lorenzo Paredes interview, March 15, 2000.
84. Paredes interview, September 22, 1994.
85. Delbert Runyon, Interview with author, November 21, 2003, Brownsville, Texas.
86. Delbert Runyon interview, November 21, 2003.
87. Paredes interview, September 22, 1994.

88. Paredes interview, September 22, 1994.
89. Américo Paredes, Introduction, *With His Pistol in His Hand* (Austin: University of Texas Press, 1958).
90. Américo Paredes, Letter to Louis Cortez, August 17, 1953, Paredes Papers.
91. Américo Paredes, Introduction, *With His Pistol.*
92. Américo Paredes, Introduction, *With His Pistol.*
93. Américo Paredes, Introduction, *With His Pistol.*
94. Américo Paredes, Introduction, *With His Pistol.*
95. Américo Paredes, Introduction, *With His Pistol.*
96. Américo Paredes, *A Texas-Mexican Cancionero: Folksongs of the Lower Border* (Urbana: University of Illinois Press, 1976), 64–67.
97. Paredes interview, September 22, 1994.
98. Paredes interview, September 22, 1994.
99. Frank H. Wardlaw, Letter to Américo Paredes, January 14, 1956, Paredes Papers.
100. Paredes interview March 25, 1995.
101. Américo Paredes, Letter to Cleotilde Paredes, September 8, 1957, Paredes Papers.
102. Cleotilde Paredes, Letter to Américo Paredes, July 2, 1958, Paredes Papers.
103. Américo Paredes, Letter to Cleotilde Paredes, July 10, 1958, Paredes Papers.
104. Paredes interview March 25, 1995.
105. Paredes interview March 25, 1995.
106. Alurista, Letter to Américo Paredes, March 6, 1978, Paredes Papers.
107. George Sánchez, Letter to Frank H. Wardlaw, April 30, 1959, Paredes Papers.
108. Américo Paredes, Letter to Charles Cumberland, March 17, 1959, Paredes Papers.
109. Thomas Sutherland, Review of *With His Pistol, The Texas Observer,* February 24, 1959, 8.
110. Gerald Ashford, Letter to Américo Paredes, January 25, 1959, Paredes Papers.
111. W. E. Simeone, Review of *With His Pistol in His Hand, Southern Illinois University Journal,* 1958, 37. Copy found in Paredes Papers.
112. Jimmie Cox, "Mexican Hero Ballad Told in Story Form," *Fort Worth Star-Telegram,* Feb. 1, 1959. Copy found in Paredes Papers.

113. Alan Paredes, Interview with author, December 9, 2001, Austin, Texas.

114. Nicanor Torres, Folksong collected in Brownsville, August 2, 1954, Paredes Papers.

115. Américo Paredes, Letter to Amelia Paredes, September 16, 1962, Paredes Papers.

116. Américo Paredes, Letter to Amelia Paredes, September 16, 1962, Paredes Papers.

117. Américo Paredes, Letter to Nena Paredes, September 7, 1962, Paredes Papers.

118. Américo Paredes, Letter to Nena Paredes, September 10, 1962, Paredes Papers.

119. Américo Paredes, Letter to Nena Paredes, September 19, 1962, Paredes Papers.

120. Américo Paredes, Letter to Nena Paredes, September 10, 1962, Paredes Papers.

121. Américo Paredes, "Questionaire–1962–1963," 1962, Paredes Papers.

122. Américo Paredes, Letter to Nena Paredes, September 10, 1962, Paredes Papers.

123. Américo Paredes, Letter to Alan Paredes, September 13, 1962, Paredes Papers.

124. Américo Paredes, Letter to Nena Paredes, January 30, 1967, Paredes Papers.

125. Américo Paredes, Letter to Lorenzo Paredes, November 19, 1963, Paredes Papers.

126. Américo Paredes, Letter to Lorenzo Paredes, November 19, 1963, Paredes Papers.

127. Vince Paredes, Interview with author, December 9, 2001, Austin, Texas.

128. *Austin American-Statesman*, Obituaries, July 24, 1999, 6.

129. Américo Paredes, Letter to Amelia Paredes, August 3, 1962, Paredes Papers.

130. Amelia Paredes, Letter to Américo Paredes, January 28, 1967, Paredes Papers.

131. Vince Paredes interview, December 9, 2001.

132. Vince Paredes interview, December 9, 2001.

133. Vince Paredes, Interview with author, August 9, 2004, Austin, Texas.
134. Vince Paredes interview, December 9, 2001.
135. Vince Paredes interview, December 9, 2001.
136. Vince Paredes interview, December 9, 2001.
137. Vince Paredes interview, December 9, 2001.
138. Vince Paredes interview, December 9, 2001.
139. Vince Paredes interview, December 9, 2001.

Notes to Chapter 5

140. Vince Paredes interview, December 9, 2001.
141. Vince Paredes interview, December 9, 2001.
142. Copies of Américo Paredes syllabi, 1974, courtesy of Francis Terry.
143. Carmen Lomas Garza, Letter to Américo Paredes, June 27, 1971, Paredes Papers.
144. Américo Paredes, Letter to Jim McNutt, June 23, 1982, Paredes Papers.
145. Américo Paredes, Letter to Jim McNutt, June 23, 1982.
146. Américo Paredes, Letter to James McNutt, March 31, 1995, Box 67, Folder 1, Paredes Papers.
147. Rolando Hinojosa, Biographical Essay about Américo Paredes, 2000, 2. Copy in Author's possession.
148. Quoted in Roberto González, "Paredes Remembered as Friend, Mentor Who Broke Down Academic Barriers for Hispanics," *The Brownsville Herald,* May 9, 1999.
149. Quoted in Roberto González, "Paredes Remembered."
150. Richard Flores, Interview with author, March 3, 2002, Austin, Texas.
151. Richard Flores interview.
152. Richard Flores interview.
153. Victor J. Guerra, ed., *En Memoria de Américo Paredes 1915–1999* (Austin: University of Texas at Austin Center for Mexican American Studies, 1999), 11.
154. Emilio Zamora, Interview with author, July 26, 2003, Austin, Texas.
155. Emilio Zamora interview.
156. José Angel Gutiérrez, Interview with author, July 27, 2001, Brownsville, Texas.

157. José Angel Gutiérrez interview, July 27, 2001.

158. José Angel Gutiérrez interview, July 27, 2001.

159. Américo Paredes, "The Mexican Contribution to Our Culture," *The Texas Observer*, August 12, 1963. Copy found in Paredes Papers.

160. Lorenzo Paredes, Interview with author, March 15, 2000, Brownsville, Texas.

161. Lorenzo Paredes interview, March 15, 2000.

162. Paredes interview, September 22, 1994.

163. Paredes interview, September 22, 1994.

164. Américo Paredes, "The Ancestry of Mexico's Corridos: A Matter of Definitions," *The Journal of American Folktale* (1963): 233. Copy found in Paredes Papers.

165. Américo Paredes, *Folklore and Culture on the Texas-Mexican Border* (Austin: University of Texas at Austin Center for Mexican American Studies, 1993), 49–51.

166. Américo Paredes, *Folklore and Culture*, 67–68.

167. Frances Terry, Interview with author, December 10, 2001, Austin, Texas.

168. Frances Terry interview, December 10, 2001.

169. Frances Terry interview, December 10, 2001.

170. Richard Dorson, Foreword, *Folktales of Mexico*, by Américo Paredes (Chicago: University of Chicago Press, 1970), xi.

171. Américo Paredes, *Folktales of Mexico*, 27. This particular version was collected by Jacob Pimentel S. in San Cristóbal de las Casas, Chiapas, on thirty-five, a schoolteacher, who learned it in Colonia de Yuquín, Simojevel, Chiapas.

172. Américo Paredes, *Folktales of Mexico*, 202.

173. Américo Paredes, *Folktales of Mexico*, 152–53.

174. Américo Paredes, *Folktales of Mexico*, back cover.

175. José Limón, Interview with author, December 10, 2001, Austin, Texas.

176. José Limón interview, December 10, 2001.

177. Américo Paredes, "Commencement Address," Texas Southmost College, May 13, 1982, Paredes Papers.

178. Américo Paredes, Foreword, *Toward New Perspectives in Folklore*, by Américo Paredes and Richard Bauman (Austin: University of Texas Press, 1972).

179. Américo Paredes, "Draft of Crystal City Baccalaureate Talk," May 1975, Paredes Papers.

180. Américo Paredes, *A Texas Mexican Cancionero*, xvii.

181. Américo Paredes, *A Texas Mexican Cancionero*, 70–71.

182. Américo Paredes, *A Texas Mexican Cancionero*, 100–2.

183. Bake Sale Flyer for Mariachi Paredes de Tejastitlán fundraiser, November 7, 1977, Paredes Papers.

184. Américo Paredes, Letter to Laverne Hinojosa, December 15, 1977, Paredes Papers.

185. José Limón, "With Corrido in His Heart," *Nuestro* (Fall 1979): 42. Copy found in Paredes Papers.

186. Américo Paredes, "The Where and Why of Folklore," *Illinois Folklore,* January 1970, 76. Copy found in Paredes Papers.

187. Américo Paredes, "The Where and Why of Folklore," 76.

188. Américo Paredes, "Folklore, Lo Mexicano and Proverbs," *Aztlán* 13 (1982): 1.

189. "Américo Paredes Named to Professorship," *Newsletter, Institute of Latin American Studies UT-Austin,* April/May 1981. Copy found in Paredes Papers.

190. Charles Champlin, "'Ballad': Crossing Over More Than One," *Los Angeles Times,* September 30, 1982, 2. Copy found in Paredes Papers.

191. John L. O'Connor, "Vi: A Mexican American Legend," *New York Times,* June 29, 1982, 10. Copy found in Paredes Papers.

192. Américo Paredes, Letter to Carolyn Osborn, June 15, 1982, Paredes Papers.

193. Paredes interview, March 25, 1995.

194. Américo Paredes, "Commencement Address," 1–2, Texas Southmost College, May 13, 1982, Paredes Papers.

195. Américo Paredes, "Commencement Address," 15, Texas Southmost College, Paredes Papers.

196. Américo Paredes, Letter to Amador Paredes, October 16, 1984, Paredes Papers.

197. Alan Paredes, Interview with author, August 9, 2004, Austin, Texas.

198. Alan Paredes interview, August 9, 2004.

199. Francisco A. Lomelí, *Dictionary of Literary Biography*, "Chicano Writers," Volume 209: Third Series, http://www.lib.utexas.edu/benson/paredes/bibliography.html, p. 13. Accessed March 20, 2003.

200. Rolando Hinojosa, Introduction to *George Washington Gómez: A Mexicotexan Novel*, by Américo Paredes (Houston: Arte Público Press, 1990), 6.

201. Américo Paredes, *George Washington Gómez*, 195.

202. Américo Paredes, Prologue, *Between Two Worlds*, 9.

203. Américo Paredes, "Ahí no más," *Between Two Worlds*, 22.

204. Américo Paredes, *Between Two Worlds*, 125, 128.

205. Américo Paredes, *Between Two Worlds*, 128.

206. Américo Paredes, "Los vendidos por Santa Anna," *Between Two Worlds*, 26.

207. Américo Paredes, *Uncle Remus con chile* (Houston: Arte Público Press, 1993), 43.

208. Américo Paredes, *Uncle Remus con chile*, 41.

209. Américo Paredes, *Uncle Remus con chile*, 38, 50.

210. Richard Bauman, Foreword, *Folklore and Culture on the Texas-Mexican Border*, by Américo Paredes (Austin: University of Texas at Austin Center for Mexican American Studies, 1993), xxii–xxiii.

211. Américo Paredes, *Folklore and Culture*, 235–36.

212. Américo Paredes, *Folklore and Culture*, 109.

213. Américo Paredes, "A Cold Night," *The Hammon and the Beans and Other Stories* (Houston: Arte Público Press, 1994), 39, 41.

214. Américo Paredes, "The Gringo," *The Hammon and the Beans and Other Stories*, 51–56.

215. Ramon Saldiver, Foreword, *The Hammon and the Beans and Other Stories*, xlv–xlvi.

216. Bernice Rendón Talavares, Interview with author, October 17, 2001, Brownsville.

217. David Montejano, "In Remembrance of Américo Paredes," *The Texas Observer*, May 28, 1999, Back Page.

218. Quoted by James Agnes, "Paredes Receives Mexico's Highest Honor," *Daily Texan*, November 20, 1990, 3.

219. "UT scholar gets top Mexican honor," *Austin American-Statesman*, November 11, 1990, 11. Copy in Paredes Papers.

220. Américo Paredes, "University of Texas at Brownsville-Texas Southmost College Commencement Address," 1, 5, May 17, 1995, Paredes Papers.

221. "Paredes to Be Honored in Texas Book Festival ceremony at Capitol," *UT News* (The University of Texas at Austin), November 5, 1998, 2.

222. Margot Torres, Tribute to Dr. Américo Paredes, November 24, 1998, University of Texas at Brownsville-Texas Southmost College.

223. Margot Torres, Tribute to Dr. Américo Paredes, November 24, 1998.

224. Manfred del Castillo interview, March 22, 2000.

225. Vince Paredes, Interview with author, August 9, 2004, Austin, Texas.

226. "Old Notes," 1938, Paredes Papers.

227. Deborah Kapchan, *En Memoria de Américo Paredes 1915–1999*, ed. Victor J. Guerra (Austin: University of Texas at Austin Center for Mexican American Studies, 1999), 61.

228. Quoted in *En Memoria*, 40.

229. Quoted in *En Memoria*, 32–33.

230. Pat Jasper, Memorial Tribute to Américo Paredes, June 2, 1999.

231. Richard Bauman, Memorial Tribute to Américo Paredes, June 2, 1999.

232. Jordanna Barton, Interview with author, March 3, 2000, Austin, Texas.

233. Joe Holley, "Américo Paredes, a Pioneer in Chicano Studies Dies at 83," *New York Times*, May 7, 1999, 5A.

234. Elaine Woo, "Américo Paredes: Southwest Scholar," *Los Angeles Times*, May 7, 1999, A30.

235. "Professor Américo Paredes," *Austin American-Statesman*, May 10, 1999, 5B.

236. Américo Paredes, unpublished poem, 1985, Paredes Papers.

237. Manuel F. Medrano, *Imágenes de la frontera sur de Tejas/Images of the South Texas Frontera* (Boston, MA: Pearson Custom Publishing, 2003), 28.

238. Vince Paredes interview, August 9, 2004.

BIBLIOGRAPHY

Books and Articles

Guerra, Victor J., ed. *En Memoria de Américo Paredes 1915–1999.* Austin: University of Texas at Austin Center for Mexican American Studies, 1999.

Irby, James A. *Backdoor at Bagdad,* Monograph 53. El Paso: The University of Texas at El Paso, Texas Western Press, 1979.

Limón, José. "With Corrido in His Heart." *Nuestro* (Fall 1979).

Lomelí, Francisco A. *Dictionary of Literary Biography. "Chicano Writers" Volume 209: Third Series,* http://www.lib.utexas.edu/benson/paredes/bibliography.html.

Medrano, Manuel F. *Imágenes de la frontera sur de Tejas/Images of the South Texas Frontera.* Boston, MA: Pearson Custom Publishing, 2003.

Montejano, David. *Anglos and Mexicans in the Making of Texas, 1836–1986.* Austin: University of Texas Press, 1987.

Paredes, Américo. "The Ancestry of Mexico's Corridos: A Matter of Definitions." *The Journal of American Folklore* 76, no. 301 (July–Sept 1963): 231–35.

———. *Between Two Worlds.* Houston: Arte Público Press, 1991.

———. *Cantos de Adolescencia.* Houston: Arte Publico, 2007.

———. *Folklore and Culture on the Texas-Mexican Border.* Austin: University of Texas at Austin Center for Mexican American Studies, 1993.

―――. "Folklore, Lo Mexicano and Proverbs." *Aztlán* 13 (1982): 1–11.

―――. *Folktales of Mexico.* Chicago: University of Chicago Press, 1970.

―――. *George Washington Gómez: A Mexicotexan Novel.* Introduction by Rolando Hinojosa. Houston: Arte Público Press, 1990.

―――. *The Hammon and the Beans and Other Stories.* Houston: Arte Público Press, 1994.

―――. "The Mexican Contribution to Our Culture." *The Texas Observer,* August 12, 1963.

―――. *A Texas-Mexican Cancionero: Folksongs of the Lower Border.* Urbana: University of Illinois Press, 1976.

―――. "The Tide." *The Palmegian Yearbook.* Brownsville, TX: NP, 1933.

―――. *Toward New Perspectives in Folklore.* Foreword by Richard Bauman. Austin: University of Texas Press, 1972.

―――. *Uncle Remus con chile.* Houston: Arte Público Press, 1993.

―――. "The Where and Why of Folklore." *Illinois Folklore* (January 1970): 75–76.

―――. *With His Pistol in His Hand.* Austin: University of Texas Press, 1958.

Patterson, James. *America in the Twentieth Century.* San Diego: Harcourt Brace Jovanovich, 1989.

Sutherland, Thomas. Review of *With His Pistol in His Hand. The Texas Observer,* February 24, 1959, 8.

Zamora, Emilio, "The Américo Paredes Papers," *The Journal of South Texas* 15 (Fall 2002): 1–17.

Articles in Newspapers

Agnes, James. "Paredes Receives Mexico's Highest Honor." *Daily Texan,* November 20, 1990, 3.

"Américo Paredes Named to Professorship." *Newsletter, Institute of Latin American Studies UT-Austin,* April/May 1981.

Austin American-Statesman, Obituaries, July 24, 1999, 6.

Champlain, Charles. "Ballad: Crossing Over More Than One." *Los Angeles Times,* September 30, 1982, 2.

Cox, Jimmie. "Mexican Hero Ballad Told in Story Form." *Fort Worth Star-Telegram,* February 1, 1959.

González, Roberto. "Paredes Remembered as Friend, Mentor Who Broke Down Academic Barriers for Hispanics." *The Brownsville Herald,* May 9, 1999.

Holley, Joe. "Américo Paredes, a Pioneer in Chicano Studies Dies at 83." *New York Times,* May 7, 1999.

O'Connor, John L. "Vi: A Mexican American Legend." *New York Times,* June 29, 1982.

"Paredes to be Honored in Texas Book Festival Ceremony at Capitol." *UT News* (The University of Texas at Austin). November 5, 1998.

Paredes, Américo. "Chaplain Dalton Won't Get Cold Feet." *The G Eye Opener,* December 30, 1945.

———. "Half Million Japanese Parade in Tokyo Streets in May Day Celebration." *Pacific Stars and Stripes,* May 2, 1946.

———. "University of Texas Prints Book." *Daily Texan,* January 8, 1959.

"Professor Américo Paredes." *Austin American-Statesman.* May 10, 1999, 5B.

"UT Scholar Gets Top Mexican Honor." *Austin American-Statesman,* November 11, 1991.

Interviews Conducted by Author

Barton, Jordanna, March 3, 2000, Austin, Texas.

Beeson, William Buford, July 23, 2003, Brownsville, Texas.

del Castillo, Manfred, March 22, 2000, Brownsville, Texas.

Flores, Richard, March 3, 2002, Austin, Texas.

Gutiérrez, José Angel, July 27, 2001, Brownsville, Texas.

Limón, José, December 10, 2001, Austin, Texas.

Martínez, Narciso, November 12, 1991, La Paloma, Texas.

Medrano, Antonia November 21, 1991, Brownsville, Texas.

Paredes, Alan, December 9, 2001, Austin, Texas.

Paredes, Alan, August 9, 2004, Austin, Texas.

Paredes, Américo, September 21, 1994, Austin Texas.

Paredes, Américo, September 22, 1994, Austin, Texas.

Paredes, Américo, March 25, 1995, Austin, Texas.

Paredes, Blanca, October 7, 2003, Brownsville, Texas.

Paredes, Lorenzo, March 15, 2000, Brownsville, Texas.

Paredes, Vince, December 9, 2001, Austin, Texas.

Paredes, Vince, August 9, 2004, Austin, Texas.

Runyon, Delbert, November 21, 2003, Brownsville, Texas.

Silva, Angélica, with Cristina Ballí, September 13, 2003, Brownsville, Texas.

Talavares, Bernice Rendón, October 17, 2001, Brownsville, Texas.

Terry, Francis, December 10, 2001, Austin, Texas.

Zamora, Emilio, July 26, 2003, Austin, Texas.

Post-interview conversation with Américo Paredes and Amelia Nagamine, September 22, 1994.

Interview Conducted by Cristina Ballí

Acosta, Teresa Palomo, September 5, 2003.

Presentations

Limón, José. Paper presented at Américo Paredes Symposium, Austin, Texas, May 3, 2001.

Torres, Margot, Tribute to Dr. Américo Paredes, November 24, 1998, University of Texas at Brownsville-Texas Southmost College.

Unpublished Materials

Hinojosa, Rolando, Biographical Essay about Américo Paredes, 2002.

North of the Border Radio program on KMBH, "Chelo Silva," September 6, 2003.

Paredes, Américo, copies of 1974 syllabi, provided by Francis Terry in 2001.

Paredes, Américo, copy of 1974 graduate syllabus for folklore, provided by Francis Terry in 2001.

Archives Consulted

Américo Paredes Papers, Benson Latin American Collection, General Libraries University of Texas at Austin.

INDEX